CHINA ONE, THE LOVE OF LUXE

Strategy and Framework Development towards Chinese Young Luxury Consumers

Authored by

Elise Ran Wang

DEDICATIONS

I dedicate my dissertation work to my family and many friends. A special feeling of gratitude to my loving parents, whose words of encouragement and push for tenacity ring in my ears.

My love Ben Ge, who believes me and gives me the warm hugs.

I also dedicate this dissertation to my many friends and professors who have supported me throughout the process. I will always appreciate all they have done, especially Jinah Oh, who I always look up to as a mentor; Grace Canepa and Patti Taylor who provided expertise and guidance throughout my study in Luxury Marketing; Robert Fee who provided support from my study in Design Management with related theory /frameworks that are used through the strategy development of this study; Jennifer Johnson, my editor, who helped me on editing the written component of this book as a friend with passion and patience.

ABSTRACT

As luxury brand executives, marketers, analysts or strategists, it is very important to understand the Chinese luxury market and the Chinese luxury consumers who are driving the demand for luxury goods and leading the future direction of the luxury market. This book will provide a unique perspective through an in-depth examination of the Chinese luxury market, especially a specific group of young luxury consumers who are called the "China One," as they are the first generation born under China's "One-Child Policy" at the beginning of China's new open-economic-environment in the late 1970s. This segment of the population is a worthwhile focus for this thesis, as they will become the main luxury consumer group in China in the immediate future. This book studies China One's identity, value system, preferences and behaviors toward luxury shopping. The goal of this study is to understand the rapidly growing power of China One and their consumption in the Chinese Luxury Market through research, aiding in the development of specific frameworks based on the data and insights to provide practical strategies and recommendations directly targeting the China One luxury consumer group.

TABLE OF CONTENTS

FIGURES

Chapter 1

INTRODUCTION

Seeing myself as a luxury marketer as well as a strategist in the future, I always wanted to study the present and find that hidden window which will let me look into the future. The present is certain; the future is unknown but is also predictable. The situation is most like a howling, fast moving train – we don't know where the destination is but we can always chase and pursue the answer by looking toward the direction to which the train is leading us...

OBJECTIVES

This study is a record of the research process as well as strategy and framework development that reflect my studies on the current Chinese luxury market status, and the consumer, which will guide us toward marketing trends of the future. By studying a potential group of consumers, the "China One", those who will have purchasing power in the Chinese luxury market, the aim is to create a blueprint for the Chinese luxury market and the luxury consumer in the immediate future. Information on the present luxury market and the consumer's behavior in China will allow us to determine what will be the best strategy in the future Chinese luxury market. This study is looking at short term to intermediate term trends of social status, economic status, global environment, and luxury consumer behavior that can guide us toward understanding and planning actions based on future market strategies toward the China One group.

TERMINOLOGIES
LUXURY=?

1. "lux·u·ry" is the enjoyment of special and expensive things, particularly food and drink, clothing, and surroundings; it is a thing that is expensive and enjoyable but not essential; a pleasure or an advantage that you do not often have.[1]

The word "luxury" comes from the Latin term "luxus" which means extravagant living, sumptuousness, opulence or indulgence.[2] However, luxury is "quite a tricky term to specify because of the noticeable involvement of human element and value recognition from society".[3] Just like beauty, the meaning of luxury is somehow a subjective concept. What is luxurious for one may not match another person's definition. For some people, luxury could mean wearing a Chanel little black dress, holding a Hermès Birkin bag, or jetting off to a fantastic little vacation island to enjoy the sunset. For some people, luxury could mean having an "it" bag for daily work and enjoying a glass of vintage red wine after work. Or, for some, a Coach bag and an Apple laptop could also be seen as luxury – the definition is personal, and different for each individual. The figure 1 from LVMH shows the change of luxury items through the decades.

However, from a luxury marketing and management perspective, how might a "luxury product" be defined?

From 1900 to Today to Future – How Definitions of Luxuries change

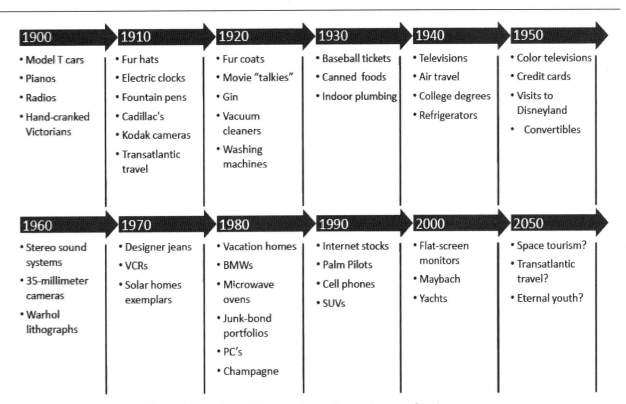

Figure 1 Changing of Representation Items of Luxury Goods

Certainly, to set up a foundation about luxury brands and their products, this is the first question that needs to be answered. The concept of luxury has been present in "divergent shapes" since the start of civilization. As Paurav Shukla mentions in his article "Defining Luxury From a Marketing Perspective": "its purpose was just as key in older western and eastern empires as it is in present day marketplace. With the unmistakable differences between social classes in earliest civilizations, the uptake of luxury was specific to the elite classes."[4] Shukla also points out that because of the acceleration of democratization, a variety of new product categories were added within the luxury market, which makes defining luxury so difficult.

Shukla uses the definition from Professor Bernard Dubo's work Luxury Possessions and Practices: an Empirical Scale: "Luxury is a unique (i.e. higher-priced) offering in almost any product or service category."[5]

One could say that a luxury brand is selective and exclusive (if that is the case); it is almost the only brand in its product category which has the most desirable attributes of being scarce, sophisticated and of good taste – however this definition seems to imperfectly define luxury. Despite the significance of knowledge gathered through marketing and the business world's practices in the past decades, "analysts and researchers still haven't arrived on a standard definition of luxury."[6]

Many experts have defined luxury in different ways; Michel Chevalier and Gerald Mazzalovo mention in their book *Luxury Brand Management* that luxury should have a strong artistic element, craftsmanship, and an international appeal that differentiates it from common products. The luxury product is a combination of the creativity from the designer and the sophistication from the craftsmen; it is an object of beauty and maintains an emotional content that leads itself to being given as a significant, valuable and memorable piece to keep in people's lives. Luxury items should have an international presence, being available in most of the world's greatest cities.[7]

Figure 2 Attributes of Luxury goods

Dr. Klaus Heine gives his opinion through his website Concept of Luxury Brands that "Luxury products have more than necessary and ordinary characteristics compared to other products of their category, which include their relatively high level of price, quality, aesthetics, rarity, extraordinariness, and symbolic meaning."[8] He believes any of the luxury brands could be evaluated by these characteristics, but defines these six characteristics as identified by the following principles shown in the figure on the left.

These defined characteristics, combined with the definition from Chevalier and Mazzalovo,[9] give a better understanding of luxury and luxury products. While Heine points out that "the modern understanding of a brand is consumer and identity oriented", Shukla also says "the underlying concept definition is customer and situation specific." Both of these opinions connect the definition of luxury to the customer and consumption which links luxury tightly back to the products. There are many ways to categorize luxury products.

Summarizing from several different approaches, here is the method that will be used in this book content and structure, including:

• Fashion: This category includes Haute Couture apparel and Ready-to-Wear apparel products (also called RTW).

Haute Couture usually remains the creation of exclusive custom-fitted clothing made-to-order for individual customers, using high-quality, expensive fabrics sewn with extreme attention to details, time-consuming fittings and hand-executed techniques.

Ready-to-wear lines can branch out from Haute Couture, and RTW provides standardized sized products to meet the wider demands in the market. They use standardized patterns and factory methods for faster construction to keep costs low in order to achieve financial objectives and keep the business running smoothly.

• Fashion Accessories: This category includes handbags and leather goods, but also includes belts and other accessories that might be included in the "total look."

• Jewelry and Watches: The luxury jewelry and watch brands usually have self-owned factories and stores or are sold through selected jewelers or department stores.

• Perfumes and Cosmetics are also considered a part of luxury goods even though they are sold at a lower price-points. This category is usually sold through large-scale distribution channels. Products from this category are the most accessible luxury goods in the field.

• The Wines and Spirits category is not the most obvious and is closely related to price. Not all wine and beverages can be called luxury goods; only those that have a high level of sophistication and are in a comparable price-range to the luxury price structure.

• Luxury Automobiles is growing interest in this segmentation of luxury goods' consumption. A luxury automobile usually carries a high-price while maintaining the value of high quality and sophistication as well as technology within the design.

• Luxury Hotels and Tourism is a unique category that is mostly related to the customer experience and exclusive hospitality service. Brand image, price-range, uniqueness of service and tour design are the main attributes when people consider luxury hotels and tourism.

• Experiential Luxuries refer to the activities that are highly exclusive experiences in different fields to the customer who pays more than the average price and asks for premium level service.

• The new luxury goods: With the fast development of technology in modern society, some new types of electronic products are considered luxury from their price structure and target customer segments. Examples are the Apple Retina Display laptop, Vertu Cellphone, or Bose multi-media home theater system. This category has not been included in the traditional sectors of luxury goods but has been considered as a new luxury sector in the modern luxury market.

Chapter two, "Open Sesame – Review of Global Luxury Market and Its Consumers", will summarize the information from secondary research which will cover the overview of the global luxury market, major players, trends, the classical theory of luxury consumption and segmentations. By studying theory reviews, data analysis, document summaries and case studies, the reader will have a clear understanding of the current status of the global luxury market which builds the foundation for the next chapter.

CHINA=?

This thesis concentrates only on Mainland China.

WHY CHINA?

Through research for this thesis, much evidence has been found that shows the significance of a study on the Chinese luxury market.

Along with the growing economy in China, there is an expanding high-income population in Mainland China, which influences the growth of the luxury market in China. The data speaks for itself - Mckinsey's Quarterly, published on Oct 2011, points out that "even during the global recession in 2009, sales of luxury goods in the mainland rose by 16 percent, to about 64 billion RMB —down from the 20 percent growth of previous years but far better than the performance of many other major luxury markets. In 2010, China's total consumption of luxury goods increased by 37 percent year-to-year to over RMB210 billion ($35 billion). China will account for about 20 percent, or 180 billion RMB ($27 billion), of global luxury sales in 2015."[10]

Researchers, consultants, and journalists all over the world have reported on the Chinese luxury market, from internal motivation studies to future marketing trends such as Chinese consumer behavior, strategy planning at luxury companies, the business model, and promotion proposals – these are all because of the importance of the Chinese Luxury Market.

Moreover, an article in Bloomberg.com titled "Chinese Shoppers Overtake U.S. as Top Luxury Buyers"[11] has announced the results of Bain & Co's research showed in the year of 2012. Chinese luxury customers had generated 25 percent of global sales through purchases in mainland China and overseas.

The November 2012 issue of *Harvard Business Review*[12] reported an interview with Francois Pinault, the CEO of PPR Group, Francois said during the review that PPR's revenues in China would likely triple by 2020.

Chinese consumers have a profound belief that they now deserve luxury products. They had fifty years with so little, and now, many can afford to buy luxury goods. Their growth in demand is rooted in an expression of individualism in the way you dress. It is a way to differentiate yourself from friends and neighbors. Chinese consumers buy to treat themselves. This China market has evolved faster than any other market in the world.[13]

KPMG has given out a report, which studied China's luxury market. The report, entitled "The Global Reach of China Luxury", points out that they have seen a "continued rise in popularity of experiential luxury consumption in Chinese luxury market" as well as a "stronger status motivation for luxury goods."[14] This gives confidence in the growing luxury market and also points out that it is "not without its challenges".[15] Studying closely and following the current market activities will help all the major luxury brands to understand the situation and then plan a future marketing strategy.

The President and CEO of Christian Dior, Sidney Toledano, wrote the foreword for the book *Luxury Brand Management*. He points out: "Because China will become in a few years the number one market in the world, given its large population and the growing buying power of the Chinese. It will become a very strong market for top European brands". He also mentions "It is obvious that China is becoming more than just a luxury market. It will develop into a major source of new brands, and new products."[16]

The comments from Luxury Brand's executives also represent how luxury brands are recognizing the importance of the Chinese market. Acknowledging the potential of the Chinese luxury market, there are many examples of marketing activities that luxury brands have implemented in the past three years, putting the "Chinese luxury market as a priority status" strategy into action.

• In 2009, brands like Chanel and Prada targeted China as their prioritized market for "China-colization"; also Chanel's "Paris-Shanghai" fashion show made a statement about its Shanghai-centric approach to the China market; Prada designed outfits for staff in the Italian Pavilionat at the Shanghai World Expo as well.

• In the same year,2009, Hermes launched its China – exclusive brand "Shang Xia" in Shanghai and won Chinese people's hearts.

• "Chinese gift for Chinese Market": In the year 2010, also known as the 'Year of the Dragon' in Chinese astrology, there were many luxury brands which designed and promoted special collections to celebrate the Chinese New Year of the Dragon. As for the latest figures, China is the world's fastest growing market of luxury goods consumption, making it ideally a hunting ground for brands such as Rolls Royce, Piaget, Versace, and Aston Martin

BRAND	Product	Price
Swarovski	Crystal statue	$20,000
L'Essence de Courvoisier du	Dragon cognac	$5,000
Versace	Year of the dragon' handbag	$5,017
Piaget	'Exceptional piece' Year of the dragon watch	$1.2 million
Parmigiani Le Dragon et La Perle du	Savoir clock	$3.5 million
Dartz Prombron	Year of the dragon edition	$7.93 million
Aston Martin	Dragon 88 range of cars	---------
Vertu	Signature dragon phone	$26,800
Blancpain	Limited Edition "Chinese Dragon" Caruso Watch	$219,682
Roberto Coin Dragon Ring and Bangle	---------------	
Zannetti Dragon watch winder	---------------	
Shanghai Tang Nespresso coffee set	---------------	

Figure 3 The Year of Dragon Limited Editions

who have created many special products for their wealthy Chinese customers. In the website BORNRICH, an article named "Top 13 luxury brands 'Year of the Dragon' editions for the wealthy Chinese"[17] also shows how the luxury brands have seen the Chinese market as the most important market. The products are shown in figure 3 above.

Chapter Three - "Into the Hundred Billion Dollar Business – Current Chinese Luxury Market and the Consumer", will provide an overview of the Chinese luxury market, major players, best practices, trends and segmentations from the secondary research. From the research, the reader will have an up to date idea of the current status of the Chinese luxury market and its consumer.

CHINA ONE=?

WHO'S THE CHINA ONE?

Unlike other countries who use Gen X, Y and Z to refer to different generations, the Chinese use different ways to segment their population by the decade in which they were born. Each group has vivid characteristics of each specific decade which I will introduce and discuss more in Chapter Three.

The Post-80s (also the Post-1980, Chinese:八零后; pinyin: bālínghòu) is a colloquial term which refers to the generation whose members were born between 1980 to 1989 in Mainland China. This generation currently ranges in age from 24 to 34 and makes up a major portion of China's young adult demographic nowadays (by the time of the book is published).

The Post-80s is the first generation in China after the introduction of the One-child Policy, and so, they have being given a unique name, The "China One".

BACKGROUND OF CHINA'S ONE-CHILD POLICY

The One-Child Policy (officially translated as "Family Planning Policy") restricts urban couples to only one child, while allowing additional children in some cases; this includes twins, rural couples, ethnic minorities, and couples who were both only children themselves. According to a report by the Chinese Population Control Department, the earth's population is increased by 160 people every minute.[18] China is the home of more than 20% of the total population in the world, which makes it play an important role in helping the stabilization of world population growth. In order to alleviate the social, economic and environmental problems caused by population issues, the Chinese government introduced the "Family Planning Policy" in 1979, which is better known as the "One-child Policy."

As the first generation of the-only-child under the One-child Policy, the "China One" have faced many new situations, such as influences from western culture, in addition to having been given more purchasing power in the families as they grow up to young adults. China One's behavior and social activities show the basic cultural interpretation of research objective. Summarize detailed information, news, and cases that relate to the One-Child

Policy with be discussed in Chapter Four.

NOTES

1. "Oxford Learner's Dictionaries." Oxford Learner's Dictionaries, n.d, http://www.oxfordlearnersdictionaries.com/us/.2012.

2. "Latin Dictionary," Latin Dictionary, n.d. http://www.latin-dictionary.org/luxus,%202006., 2012

3. Paurav Shukla, "Defining Luxury from a Marketing Perspective," n.d. http://ezinearticles.com/?Defining-Luxury-From-a-Marketing-Perspective&id=4944155. 2009.

4. Ibid.

5. Bernard Dubois and Gilles Laurent ,"Luxury Possessions and Practices: An Empirical Scale," in *E - European Advances in Consumer Research*, Vol. 2, ed. Flemming Hansen (Provo, UT : Association for Consumer Research, 1995), 69-77. Shukla.

6. Shukla.

7. Micheal Chevalier, and Gerald Mazzalove, *Luxury Brand Management (A World of Privilege)* (Holooken,NJ:John Wiley & Sons, 2008), 117.

8. "The Definition of Luxury Brands," accessed March 24, 2014, http://www.conceptofluxurybrands.com/concept/luxury-brands-definition.

9. Chevalier and Massalovo,119.

10. "Tapping China's Luxury-goods Market | McKinsey & Company," accessed March 24, 2014, http://www.mckinsey.com/insights/marketing_sales/tapping_chinas_luxury-goods_market.

11. Vinicy Chan, "Chinese Shoppers Overtake U.S. as Top Luxury Buyers," Bloomberg, December 12, 2012, http://www.bloomberg.com/news/2012-12-12/chinese-shoppers-overtake-u-s-as-top-luxury-buyers.html.

12. Michael J. Silverstein, "Don't Underestimate China's Luxury Market," *Harvard Business Review*, December 12, 2012, accessed March 24, 2014, http://blogs.hbr.org/2012/12/chinas-luxury-market-and/.

13. Ibid.

14. Global Reach of China Luxury, KPMG, n.d.accessed March 24,2014,http://www.kpmg.com/Global/en/IssuesAndInsights/ArticlesPublications/Documents/global-reach-china-luxury.pdf.

15. Ibid.

16. Chevalier,119.

17. "Top 13 Luxury Brands 'Year of the Dragon' Editions for the Wealthy Chinese | Bornrich," accessed March 24, 2014, http://www.bornrich.com/top-13-luxury-brands-year-dragon-editions-wealthy-chinese.html.

18. "Family Planning in China," Family Planning in China, 2012, accessed March 24, 2014, http://www.lawinfochina.com/display.aspx?lib=dbref&id=7.

Chapter 2

OPEN SESAME!
– Global Luxury Market Overview

"Open Sesame" comes from the story of Ali Baba and the Forty Thieves in the book "1001 Nights." This magical phrase opens the gate of a cave filled with treasures. Taking a panoramic view of the global luxury market, it's just like a cave full of golden coins, priceless jewels as well as unpredictable secret discoveries. These two words are the key that will reveal the hidden luxury market nuances, the environmental elements as well as the hearts of its consumers...

THE EXTERNAL CONTRIBUTORS OF THE GLOBAL LUXURY MARKET

The global luxury market is not running by itself; on the contrary, it is affected and influenced by many sectors in the global market environment. These sectors are the global economic situation, cultural background, trends and innovations in art and design, latest developments in technology as well as ecological issues and status. The key to predicting global trends in the luxury market is to reveal the contributions the aforementioned sectors are having on the global luxury market's growth.

INDIRECT GLOBAL ECONOMIC IMPACT

The International Monetary Fund projects economic global growth at 3.3 and 3.6 percent in 2012 and 2013. There are many reasons behind the projection, such as:

• The crisis in the Euro Zone

• Output and employment weakened again in the United States

• Domestic demand continues to lose momentum

• Sluggish prospects and bumpy growth

• Fiscal adjustment will continue but not in many countries

• Relatively solid emerging market economies

But how will the economic status influence the luxury market's performance?

All in all, economic activity is forecast to remain tepid in many economies. According to Seung Yoon Rhee "the recovery is forecast to limp along in the major advanced economies, with growth remaining at a fairly healthy level in many emerging markets and developing economies."[1] She also points out that even though the global economy is still recovering from depression, the luxury market, on the other hand, is climbing steadily year after year.

By examining the figure 4 on the next page, you can see that there is no a clear-cut relationship between economic environment and the luxury market's performance.

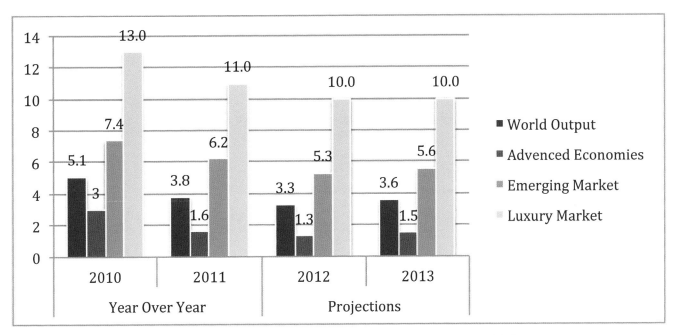

Figure 4 Comparing the Global Economy and the Global Luxury Market

CULTURAL DYNAMICS INFLUENCING LUXURY PURCHASES

Cultural values and social status in different countries could be considered as synergistically connected to the drivers of luxury consumers' purchasing behavior. These dynamics are the power pushing the growth of luxury consumption.

One example in western culture is Kate Middleton's wedding dress. The luxury fashion house of Alexander McQueen designed the bridal gown. With the many great reviews about the design of the wedding dress, Alexander McQueen, as a national brand in Britain, earned much more attention from European luxury consumers. Kate Middleton's royal wedding not only influenced fashion trends, but luxury goods consumption growth as well. Because of the social status and prominence of Kate Middleton, her wedding dress choice and the brand value of Alexander McQueen are perfect examples of cultural dynamics meeting social status.

This phenomenon is not only happening in western cultures, but also in eastern cultures as well. For example, in China, politicians are viewed as holding a higher social status as well as being in a higher economic scale. It is also customary for politicians to give and receive luxury goods during their political day-to-day endeavors. It is also a sign of prominence. Therefore, it is not only a symbol of wealth but also a sign of social status not just among politicians but also among society in general. In the article "Chinese Politics and the Rise of Understated Luxury," it is mentioned that ".... Government officials drive China's luxury market... "[2] In another article, "China Luxury Sales to Get Boost After Leadership Change," it is argued that "Luxury companies are betting that Chinese shoppers who are buying fewer gold bars and lavish gifts for their business dealings will loosen their purse strings after a once-a-decade government change in Beijing."[3] These examples show how social status can become an influential effort of luxury consumption.

Similar to China, as an emerging country, India's luxury market is continuously growing. India's luxury market is projected to reach USD 14.7 billion in 2015.[4] Indians are highly accustomed to a multiplicity of traditional festivals and large family structures based on the history

Figure 5 LV Speedy bags from Stephen Sprouse's collection

of India as well as its large population. This social status makes gifting an important part of its culture. This significance gives luxury companies a great way to promote their products as luxurious gift choices.[5] The cultural dynamics in India have become not only an influence of luxury purchasing, but also a motivation of luxury goods consumption in Indian minds.

From either the developed western or the emerging eastern luxury markets, these examples have shown the influence of cultural background and social status as a definite driver of global luxury market growth.

THE EVOLVING MARRIAGE OF ART AND DESIGN

Since the 1920's, the Luxury segment has demonstrated good examples of collaboration, such as Salvador Dalí creating dresses for Coco Chanel and Elsa Schiapparelli. In the 1930's, Ferragamo commissioned designs for advertisements from Futurist painter Lucio Venna for his shoes. Later, Gianni Versace commissioned works from Alighiero Boetti and Roy Lichtenstein for the launch of his name collections.[6]

Over the past decade, collaboration between the luxury industry and artists has built up a revolutionary and unique partnership, from product development to promotion and branding. Nowadays, major luxury brands have started to see the benefits of working with artists to work on innovative and artistic designs for their products. Yves Carcelle, the President and CEO of Louis Vuitton, said: "Luxury and art are both expressions of emotion and passion; therefore, the idea of integrating artwork in a store environment is a question of affinity."[7] In the last few years, Louis Vuitton has collaborated with many contemporary artists throughout the world, such as the earlier collaborations with Stephen Sprouse [as Figure 5 shows]; for both Fall 2006 and 2008, LV utilized Sprouse's 1987 graffiti leopard images for handbags, shoes, and scarves for Louis Vuitton, which sold out instantly. After one year, Louis Vuitton promoted its new Rose Collection designed by Sprouse which once again showed a great success in sales.

Collaboration between Japanese artist Takashi Murakami and Vuitton creative director Marc Jacobs resulted in the Multicolore, Cherry Blossom, and Cerises lines of Murakami bags that were featured in the spring 2003 show. Limited-edition product shipments were all pre-sold; the waiting list reached the tens of thousands; and estimated sales of the collection were $345 million, about 10 percent of Vuitton's total revenues.

In 2011, LV invited artist Yayoi Kusama to create a collection for the company. The collaboration went from being limited to offering product design and development toward a wider range of fields, such as branding, packaging design, store display as well as visual merchandising. Yayoi Kusama worked with creative director Marc Jacobs (who visited her studio in Japan in 2006) on a collection of Louis Vuitton products by using her famous polka dots. The collection included leather goods, ready-to-wear, accessories, shoes, watches, and jewelry [See Figure 6]. While the collection was available in major stores of Louis Vuitton, the interior displays as well as the window designs reflected Kusamas's art. LVMH's revenue report for the first three quarters of 2012 indicates the fashion

category of luxury sales grew by eight percent. One of the reasons is the launch of Yayoi Kusama's collection.[8]

The above examples show the evolution of how fashion and luxury companies gain inspiration from art or directly collaborate or have gone from design of product to the whole business and marketing strategy level.

CRAFTSMANSHIP MEETS TECHNOLOGY

Just as art, the long-term trends in the global luxury industry are also driven by the latest and most updated technology. New materials merge with the old, and new needs drive innovation, while luxury brands are trying everything to excite their customers. Which of today's myriad of technological trends are driving the luxury brands of today and tomorrow?

Burberry is the first fashion brand to live-stream its runway shows, the first to sell live from the catwalk on-line and in-store via iPad, and the one and only brand to attempt a 3D holographic film immersion for its China launch.[9] Burberry is the most digitally advanced luxury and fashion brand listed in the top 20 most innovative companies in the world. Burberry sees "Digital innovation," the contribution of technology development, as part of its focused execution of

Figure 6 LV Yayoi Kusama Collection and Store Layout

key strategies.[10] Usage of technology has helped Burberry not only on runway shows, but has also consistently generated revenue. Since 2010, revenue has increased from $1185 million to $1501 million in 2011 and closed at $1857 million in 2012.[11]

In September 2012, at New York Fashion Week, there were several major technology driven fashion shows as well. The designers used high technology innovative fabric, used social media to communicate with audience with the first hand information of the show, also got feedback before or during the runway show to ensure their design is well received by the audience.

As the younger generation, who grew up with technological devices, gains greater purchasing power, technology has evolved from nearly cool gadgets into the key to sustainable growth and survival amidst competition. Technology was become the basic premise towards keeping products updated and functional and connecting to the consumer who communicates, shares information, and shops in the digital world.

The above approach makes Burberry a standout in the luxury business, which has historically shied away from technology for fear of eroding its aura of exclusivity. The biggest thing they have done differently is to put a relentless focus on digital innovation.

THE GREEN DENIAL

If the digital evolution is the development driver of the of the luxury market, then sustainability will be the key to survival. Nowadays, fashion brands are starting to hold themselves directly responsible for the health of the global environment. One good example is Levis Strauss & Co. who has continually supported environmentalism and social responsibility. Many luxury brands, on the other hand, haven't put much effort into the development of sustainability yet, which has an impact on their marketing performance because of the ever-changing shopping behavior of the customer.

The World Wildlife Fund proposes that the emergence of a new kind of luxury consumer is one who is well heeled, educated, and concerned about social and environmental issues, and one who uses luxury products as a symbol of success. Many successful people now expect the brands they support to reflect their own concerns and aspirations for a better world.

In short, the luxury industry has to evolve and integrate sustainability into their business strategies, or die. Only then can we redefine what "luxury" means: a term that is synonymous with quality, timelessness, as well as social and environmental excellence.[12]

Arguably, no one has done more to spread the gospel of green than Stella McCartney, whose mission continues to oppose leather and fur and whose Fall 2012 collection featured platform soles made out of bio-degradable material and is set to launch a hot new line of sunglasses from castor oil seeds.

The Valentino Fashion Group has promised that by January 2020 that it will get rid of all hazardous chemicals that are currently associated with its production process. They have even agreed to a zero deforestation policy on leather and packaging procurement.[13]

While Valentino may have been at the top of the class, other brands have not paid enough attention. Greenpeace Italy has released a Sustainability Evaluation Ranking for 2012 for high-end French and Italian fashion brands. The grade was derived from the examination of leather, pulp and paper, and toxic water pollution. Due to their current practices, brands such as Dior, Gucci, and Louis Vuitton were graded as "poor." Brands such as Chanel, Prada, , and Hermès outright failed because of their failure to provide information for the Greenpace Survey.

The call is for luxury brands to connect with their customers who are increasingly aware and eco-conscious by making green marketing a part of their strategy. The luxury brands are expected to give back to society and support ethical production. The customer, based on their purchasing decisions, will measure this outlook.

THE OVERVIEW OF WORLD LUXURY MARKET

THE GROWTH OF LUXURY MARKET IN 2012 – 2013

The world is truly global, and the luxury sector reflects this as brands cross - geographic boundaries to reach consumers all over the world. Moderate growth in the U.S. and European markets, coupled with strong performance in emerging markets, are driving growth in all the luxury goods sectors. With ever-changing technologies, social media evolution, and a refined and informed generation of millennial consumers, the meaning of luxury is being redefined.[14]

The nature of growth is shifting substantially in seven key ways during the year of 2012 to 2013:

1. Chinese customers who make up half of the luxury purchases in all of Asia have further transformed the luxury market with growth in domestic sales and continued voracious spending as tourists. Globally, one in four purchases of personal luxury goods comes from Chinese consumers.

2. E-commerce is continuing to grow at 25 percent a year, while sales at off-price (i.e., discount) outlets will see 30 percent growth. Together, these emerging channels amount to €20 billion, effectively the equivalent of sales in Japan.

3. There is a generational shift under way as young consumers seek significantly different experiences from luxury consumption, seeking uniqueness over heritage. For them, a luxury goods shopping experience is 24/7 access over exclusivity, and entertainment over mere shopping.

4. Accessories have become the core category in luxury goods consumption. This year is the first time that leather goods and shoes have become the largest piece of the market, now at 27 percent of sales. The category is showing increasing levels of male spending, and increasing interest in higher quality, higher price items.

5. Tourists now account for 40 percent of global luxury spending. As tourism and luxury spending becomes more tightly intertwined, the experiential dimension of luxury consumption becomes as critical for brands to deliver as their products.[15]

MAJOR PLAYERS

The top 10 most valuable luxury fashion brands in 2013 are Hermes, Chanel, Louis Vuitton , Christian Dior, Ferragamo, Versace, Prada, Fendi , Giorgio Armani , and Ermenegildo Zegna.

THE "BIG THREES"

The fashion luxury market is dominated by three major players: LVMH, Richemont and PPR. By reviewing their revenue, corporate structure, mission statement as well as their recent activities, we can peek into their operations and get a glance as to how they continue to dominate the market.

1. LVMH

LVMH Moët Hennessy • Louis Vuitton S.A., known as LVMH, is a French international luxury goods corporation based in Paris, France. The company was founded after the merger of Louis Vuitton and Moët Hennessy in 1987.[16] LVMH is the strongest player in the luxury goods industry, a giant in an industry where fixed costs make scale paramount, the only "two legged" balanced player who leads with mega-brands in both Fashion and Wines & Spirits.

LVMH just reported great results for 2012. Revenues increased 19 percent to €28.1 Billion (roughly $37.7 Billion). Earnings increased 12% to €3.4 Billion (about $4.6 Billion). The strong results were due to top performances by many brands including Louis Vuitton, Bulgari and Moët Hennessy. Performance was especially strong in Asia as well as the United States.

The mission of the LVMH group is to represent the most refined qualities of Western "Art de Vivre" around the world. LVMH must continue to be synonymous with both elegance and creativity. The products, and the cultural values they embody, blend tradition and innovation and kindle dream and fantasy.[17]

There are some of the recent key developments of LVMH:
• LVMH is focused on strengthening its jewelry and watches proposition
• Salvatore Ferragamo has collaborated with Bulgari to create the former's first jewelry range
• LVMH is to celebrate its craftsmanship and heritage
• Bulgari opened a luxury hotel in London

• LVMH's share of revenues from Asia Pacific, excluding Japan, has been growing rapidly

2. RICHMONT

Compagnie Financière Richemont SA is a Switzerland-based luxury goods holding company founded in 1988 by South African businessman Johann Rupert. Through its various subsidiaries, Richemont designs, manufactures, distributes and sells fashion and accessories, premium jewelry, watches, leather goods, as well as writing instruments. The brands under Richemont included Cartier, Van Cleef & Arpels, Piaget, Vacheron Constantin, Jaeger-LeCoultre, IWC, Alfred Dunhill, and Montblanc which represent a tradition of style, quality and craftsmanship. The Net-a-Porter, on the other hand, is an innovation of its marketing activities, which has produced outstanding sales in the on-line commerce category.

The mission of Richemont Group is committed to preserving high standards of performance and unsurpassed quality in everyday business activities. They see it as a privilege to work for, and represent, excellence, tradition and prestige. They conduct business in accordance with management principles that place value in people's successes, namely: trust, loyalty, and mutual respect.

An announcement in January, the Group's operating profit is significantly higher than the prior year: at €2040 million, it is 51 percent above last year's level.

Some of the recent key developments of Richmont are:
• Richemont is keen to grow its supply of premium watches
• Richemont has announced plans to boost its capital expenditure
• Van Cleef & Arpels introduced its exquisite Bals de Légende collection
• Richemont continues to buy back its equity
• Net-A-Porter has launched a dedicated proposition for men and beauty products

3. PPR

PPR (previously known as Pinault-Printemps-Redoute when founded in 1963), is a French multinational holding company that develops a worldwide brand portfolio (luxury, sport & lifestyle divisions and retail brands) distributed in 120 countries.

The mission of PPR is to offer products that enable the customers to express their personality and to fulfill their dreams. To achieve this, PPR will empower an ensemble of powerful complementary brands to reach their full growth potential by constantly pushing them against the limits in the most imaginative and sustainable manner.[18]

Strong luxury sales outside Europe raised French retail and luxury group PPR's 2012 revenue and profits after the company behind Gucci and Yves Saint Laurent jettisoned two of its weaker brands and pressed hard into emerging markets. PPR reported that net income rose 6.3 percent to €1.4 billion as sales rose 20 percent to €9.7 billion. Sales in Asia, excluding Japan, accounted for a quarter of PPR's total — a slight increase over 2011.[19]

Here are some of the recent key developments of PPR:

• PPR has acquired a premium watchmaker

• Balenciaga has launched a transactional website

• PPR has expanded its sportswear proposition

• Christian Louboutin is seeking compensation from Yves Saint Laurent

• Bottega Veneta has opened a store dedicated for home-wares in the Middle East

• Gucci has launched eco-friendly eye-wear

• The company has increased its focus on e-commerce operations

EMERGING CONTEMPORARY BRANDS

Social media and similar venues have served as the platform for otherwise unknown designers, to become the new rising stars in this difficult to penetrate medium. We now call these rising stars, contemporary designers who gave birth to contemporary brands. This concept refers to fashion, accessories and other items that are often sold under other prestigious brands, which are commonly named after the designer. Some of these brands are Marc Jacobs, Jason Wu, and Alexander Wang.

Figure 7 Marc Jacobs Runway Show 2012

Instead of everyone wanting to have an LV bag, people now fall in love with newer and smaller contemporary brands: an Alexander Wang bag, a Marc Jacobs dress or a Jason Wu shirt. These contemporary brands are perceived as having seven defining qualities: less ostentatious, more accessible, more modern, more rational, best in class, sleeker in design, and precision in fabrication. They are not necessarily seen as inferior to luxury; however, this may not always be the case in all parts of the world.

There are several characteristics of the contemporary brand sector which makes it fairly important when predicting the future trends of the luxury market.
• Target a part of the same customer with luxury brand.
• Share the same distribution channels with the luxury brands.
• Promote with highly loyal customer's support
• Keep innovative and fast moving energy

These unique characteristics become even more important in the future, as the young luxury consumer starts to dominate the market and his thirst for luxury products increases. Who is to say that one or more of these contemporary brands will not become the next LV or Chanel in the very near future?

THE ONE-TIMERS – COLLABORATIVE PRODUCTS CROSS SECTORS

Luxury collaborations have been gaining steam in recent years, especially in these current economic conditions which favor cost-effective marketing solutions. For the luxury industry, it describes the brave new world of co-branding, which benefits not only the high end houses but also the emerging contemporary designers by providing them with increased exposure and market share. Collaboration in the luxury market is no longer a new phenomenon,

A few examples that illustrate different types of collaboration follow:

1. Luxury brands with other industry sectors – Gucci and Fiat

In 2012, Fiat launched a revamped limited edition convertible Fiat 500 with Gucci's design and leather product featured outside and inside of the car. Patrizio di Marco, the CEO of Gucci, says, "This is a car that is part of

Figure 8 Examples of Collaboration Product Lines

Italian life the same with Gucci."[20] This is a perfect description of the collaboration between Fiat and Gucci. The brands which share similar culture or values always produce collaborative products together. It is a win-win for the brands as both gain income as well as brand awareness among different sectors in the market.

2. Luxury Designer with department store – Karl Lagerfeld with Macy's

This type of collaboration benefits the designer by gaining notoriety and the department store by gaining a well-known designer. In addition, the department stores get foot traffic which in all likelihood will generate additional sales which translate into more revenue. It's a win-win when the right match is made.

3. Luxury brand with mass-production retailer – Versace with H& M

"24-hour queue"... "Sold out in 30 minutes"..."Shoppers go wild" – when searching Versace and H&M on line, these are the words that pop up first on the screen. This is one of the most successful collaborations to date. Hordes of shoppers besieged H&M stores across the globe as Versace's collection for the high street shop went on sale.[21] This is another example of how the collaboration between designer and retailer benefits both parties – Versace by gaining exposure and H&M by clearly gaining more foot traffic and revenue as illustrated by their sold out performance.

4. Contemporary brand with mass merchant retailer – Jason Wu with Target

Collaboration with designers has taken mass merchant retailing to new levels by redefining the shopping experience. A perfect example is Target's impressive list of high fashion designer partnerships, which reads like a line-up for Fashion Week – Isaac Mizrahi, Missoni, etc. Among these collections the most outstanding is Jason Wu's which went on sale last Feb of 2012 and sold out in a morning, leading its web site to crash for a week. Target's main objective for partnering with designers is to drive traffic and create a buzz.[22] Here again, the collaboration brings an otherwise emerging designer to the spot light.

CONSUMER ELECTRONICS - THE NEW LUXURY CATEGORIES

Accounting for 40 percent of global sales, men's spending on luxury also grew almost twice as fast as women's in 2011, 14 percent compared with eight percent respectively.[23] Unlike women who are more impulsive in purchasing luxury goods, men value brand equity, quality and technology in products, which has created a new category for luxury consumption, that of consumer electronics.

Consumer electronics is electronic equipment intended for everyday use, most often in entertainment, communications and office productivity. Consumer electrical products include personal computers, telephones, audio equipment, televisions, digital cameras, etc. Increasingly, these products are based on digital technologies and have largely merged with the computer industry in what is increasingly referred to as the customization of information technology.

The significant differentiation of this sector is the high price range associated with a short product life span as well as the ever-changing technology. The products also maintain customized functions according to the owner's needs and daily usage. Therefore, high-end consumer electronics are more desired by men, who are interested in technology and have a digitally oriented lifestyle. There are many companies and brands that can be considered in the high-end consumer electronic sector.[24]

Three representative brands are:

1. VERTU

Vertu is a British manufacturer and retailer of luxury mobile phones established by Finnish mobile-phone manufacturer Nokia as a wholly owned subsidiary in 1998.[25] In October 2012 Nokia sold Vertu to private equity group EQT VI for an unspecified amount (rumored to be $200 million), but will retain a 10% share. By early 2013, 326,000 phones had been sold. The phones are technologically modest and most popular in Russia, Asia and the

Middle East.

2. BOSE

The Bose Corporation is an American privately held corporation that specializes in audio equipment. Bose is known for its loudspeakers, noise-canceling headsets, and automotive sound systems. Other products manufactured by Bose include amplifiers and headphones.[26] Bose audio products distinguish the brand from the market competitors because of the strong brand image and high quality as well as the products' function and design.

3. APPLE

Apple Inc. designs, develops, and sells consumer electronics, computer software and personal computers. In 2001, with the successful introduction of the iPod and iTunes, Apple established itself as a leader of personal electronics and music devices. Also, Apple is know for its iOS system which runs in its computers, smart phones, and media players and which began with the iPhone followed by the iPod Touch and then iPad. As of 2012, Apple is the largest publicly traded corporation in the world by market capitalization, with an estimated value of US$626 billion as of September 2012.[27] Apple Inc's market cap is larger than that of Google and Microsoft combined. Apple's worldwide annual revenue in 2010 totaled US$65 billion, growing to US$127.8 billion in 2011 and $156 billion in 2012.[28]

THE OVERVIEW OF LUXURY CONSUMERS STUDY
EXISTING STUDY OF MOTIVATION OF LUXURY CONSUMPTION

Dr. Schiffman and Kanuk point out that motivation is "the driving force within individuals that leads to their actions."[29] In the study of luxury purchasing behavior, the motivation for the consumers' actions to purchase luxury goods is their unfulfilled needs or desires. Wells and Prensky[30] suggest that luxury products are treated as a tool to meet their needs and satisfy their wants. The traditional motivations for purchasing luxury brands were to "Buy to impress others." Moreover, more recent studies showed that personal orientation and identification have contributed to the increase in product consumption worldwide.[31]

Paurav Shukla, one of the few leading researchers in luxury consumption, introduced three types of antecedents in his work about the motivation behind luxury consumption.

These antecedents are: Brand, Situational and Socio-psychological. He also created two categories of motivations for luxury consumption – the "To Show" group which defines consumers as wanting to attract attention from peers and show certain status for receiving desired outcomes and the "To Feel" group which represents the consumer's need of experiencing positive emotions, feel satisfaction and reach desired state of consciousness through possession of luxury products.

From this model, we can see Shukla has proven that Luxury consumption is no longer an individual behavior but a social activity that is influenced by the dynamic of one's rational and emotional perspective as well as the social influences of status and daily life.

EXISTING STUDY OF SEGMENTATION

Because luxury consumer behavior does not abruptly change within different countries[32] the major challenge for luxury companies facing an international worldwide marketplace is to identify and satisfy the desires and needs of a wide array of luxury consumer segmentations, which requires a global common level in research methodology and models.[33] Regarded as a common denominator that can be used to define consumption across cultures[34] luxury is a main factor that differentiates a brand in a product category[35] and a central driver of consumer preference and usage.[36] The following are three widely used consumer segmentation that are often used in luxury marketing research and practices.

BCG'S SEGMENTATION

But a new report from BCG Research digs deeper to divide the luxury consumer into five distinct species. BCG surveyed six luxury markets–the U.S., Brazil, China, Japan, Russia, and Europe. They found that each of the five species has experienced the financial crisis differently. They are: [37]

1. The Aspirational. Those with $85,000 or more in annual income in developed markets or $29,000 in emerging markets account for four out of every five luxury purchases in the markets studied, according to

BCG. They aren't big spenders individually, but together they account for a third of all luxury spending. There are 115 million of these households in the studied markets.

2. Rising Middle Class. This oddly named group has incomes of $170,000 or more in the U.S. and $55,000 in emerging markets–making them have more affluent than the real "middle class." But they account for 25 percent of luxury spending in the studied markets. There are 25 million of these households in the markets studied. They spend most of their money on cosmetics and fragrances, and they like leather goods, which last longer and show their taste and social status.

3. New Money Households. The New Money crowd has investable assets of $1 million or more, and they spend about $90 billion a year on traditional luxury, or about a third of the market. There are six million of these households in the markets studied. They like fashion and clothing.

4. Old Money Households. The Old Money group inherited its money and is far more frugal, accounting for only seven percent of luxury sales. There are one million of these households in the markets studied.

5. Beyond-Money Households. This group may be self-made but it shuns status spending as ostentatious and tasteless. Their disdain for luxury brands is, in a way, an affirmation of their elite status. There are about a half million of these households. When they do spend, they spend on watches, jewelry, and furniture decorations.

GEN X<Y<Z<?

Understanding the differences between the generations is fundamental in building a successful luxury marketing strategy. Here is a brief description of each generation as follows:[38]

1. Baby Boomers: The "baby boomers" are those born in the decade following the end of World War II (aged roughly 49-67) who are considered a generation who have "had it all", cosseted by parents who experienced the Great Depression and raised in the prosperous post-war era. Many benefited from free tertiary education and relatively low housing costs. Common put-downs range from "self-obsessed" to "stuck in their ways."[39]

2. Generation X: Those born roughly between 1963-1980. Gen-Xers are often labeled the "slacker" generation, uncommitted and unfocused. The "why me?" Generation. They are the first generation to have experienced

divorce on a large scale and are likely to have changed careers several times. While their parents grew up in the era of the Civil Rights movement, Xers are considered more likely to want to keep their heads down than to change the world.

3. Generation Y: Those born between 1981 and 1994. Common put-downs include lazy, debt-ridden and programmed for instant gratification. They are portrayed as demanding and unrealistic in their career aspirations. Now we can add "Internet-addicted" and "lonely" to the list.

4. Generation Z: Those born between 1995 and 2009, they are the first generation never to have experienced the pre-internet world. Accordingly, they are already technology-focused.

5. Generation Alpha: Yes, now we're onto the Greek alphabet. This generation begins with those born in 2010. It has been predicted they will be the most formally educated generation in history, beginning school earlier and studying longer. The children of older, wealthier parents with fewer siblings, they are already being labeled materialistic.[40]

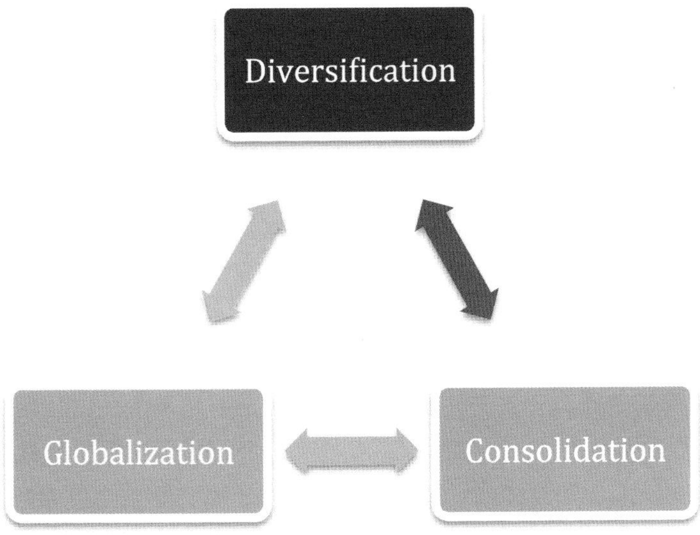

NEW FIVE TYPES OF LUXURY CONSUMER

A special feature in Unity Marketing's *Luxury Report 2012*[41] is a psycho-graphic profile of five key types of luxury consumers. These include:

1. X-Fluents (Extremely Affluent): who spend the most on luxury and are most highly invested in luxury living. In the webinar you will learn why the share of X-Fluents is on the rise in the current market, as other personality types drop out of the overall luxury market.

2. Butterflies: The most highly evolved luxury consumers who have emerged from their luxury

Figure 9 Trends of Luxury Market

cocoons with a passion to reconnect with the outside world. Powered by a search for meaning and new experiences, the Butterflies have the least materialistic orientation among the segments.

3. Luxury Coroners: who are focused on hearth and home. They spend most of their luxury budgets on home-related purchases.

4. Aspirers: those luxury consumers who have not yet achieved the level of luxury to which they aspire. They are highly attuned to brands and believe luxury is best expressed in what they buy and what they own.

5. Temperate Pragmatists, a newly emerged luxury consumer who is not all that involved in the luxury lifestyle. As their name implies, they are careful spenders and not given to luxury indulgence.

EXISTING STUDY OF SHOPPING TRENDS

The three main trends in the luxury market are globalization, consolidation, and diversification,[42] "which have acquired additional meaning amid the proliferation of social networks and emergence of collaborative luxury consumption that is representative of the current decade, especially in the years of global economic recession."[43] Globalization refers to the 24/7 customers all over the world who have many shopping choices and options of where, when, and how to shop. Consolidation involves the growth of brands and companies across all sectors. It also refers to the unification of a brand's image throughout all distribution channels. Diversification refers to the shopping behavior as it directly relates to the shopping experience. Shopping today is a 24/7 event, facilitated by the technological revolution.[44]

The rise in the number of emerging markets, particularly the BRIC countries (Brazil, Russia, India and China), have led the luxury market to branch into new channels which offer up fewer luxurious (lower price) product lines at more affordable prices. In addition, accessibility to these brands does not necessitate travel to fashion capitals of the world. Now you can buy your favorite luxury brand on-line from the comfort of your home at any time, or visit your local luxury mall and buy the product of your choice.

NOTES

1. "World Economic Outlook, October 2012: Coping with High Debt and Sluggish Growth. IMF, n.d., accessed March 24, 2014, http://www.imf.org/external/pubs/cat/longres.aspx?sk=25845.

2. "Chinese Politics and the Rise of Understated Luxury | Buy Buy China," accessed March 24, 2014, http://www.buybuychina.com/flash-crash-will-chinas-luxury-buyers-embrace-understated-designs/.

3. Vinicy Chan, "China Luxury Sales to Get Boost After Leadership Change," Bloomberg, October 31, 2012, http://www.bloomberg.com/news/2012-10-30/china-luxury-sales-to-get-boost-after-leadership-change.html.

4. "India's Luxury Market Could Reach 14,7 Billion Dollars by 2015 - New Study," CPP-LUXURY, accessed March 24, 2014, http://www.cpp-luxury.com/indias-luxury-market-could-reach-147-billon-dollars-by-2015-new-study/.

5. Kaushambi, "Emerging Luxury Trends in India for 2012!," Indian Business of Technology, Mobile & Startups, accessed March 24, 2014, http://trak.in/tags/business/2012/04/04/india-emerging-luxury-trends-2012/.

6. "The Evolving Marriage of Art and Fashion," Luxury Society, April 6, 2009. http://luxurysociety.com/articles/2009/04/the-evolving-marriage-of-art-and-fashion.

7. Ibid.

8. LVMH 2012 Annual Report, 2013, accessed March 24, 2014, http://www.lvmh.com/investor-relations/documentation/reports.

9. "Burberry: More Than the Trench Coat, It's Leading British Digital Innovation," *The Huffington Post UK*, accessed March 24, 2014, http://www.huffingtonpost.co.uk/2011/09/07/burberry-the-best-of-brit_n_951697.html.

10. Interim Results for the Six Months Ended 30 September 2012, Burberry Group, n.d., accessed March 24, 2014 http://www.burberryplc.com/documents/results/2012/interim_results/brby071112.pdf.

11. Burberry Annual Report 2012/2013, Burberry Plc, n.d., accessed March 24, 2014, http://www.burberryplc.com/investor_relations/annual_reports/financial_review.

12. Dayle Deanes, "14 Mainstream Luxury Brands That Have Flirted With Eco-Fashion | Ecouterre," accessed March 24, 2014, http://www.ecouterre.com/14-mainstream-luxury-brands-that-have-flirted-with-eco-fashion/.

13. "Greenpeace Ranks Valentino as Top Eco-Friendly Luxury Brand (Look Inside To Shop Valentino Pieces, Guilt Free)," StyleBlazer, February 9, 2013, http://styleblazer.com/127584/greenpeace-ranks-valentino-as-top-eco-friendly-luxury-brand-look-inside-to-shop-valentino-pieces-guilt-free/.

14. RobWalker, "2012: A Game Changer for Luxury Goods," Euromonitor, January 18, 2013, accessed March 24, 2014, http://blog.euromonitor.com/2013/01/2012-a-game-changer-for-luxury-goods.html.

15. Ibid.

16. "LVMH 2012 Annual Report, 2013," accessed March 24, 2014,http://www.lvmh.com/investor-relations/documentation/reports.

17. "Louis Vuitton's Vision and Mission," Louis Vuitton Unveiled, accessed March 24, 2014,http://jodiechan.weebly.com/2/post/2012/12/louis-vuittons-vision-and-mission.html.

18. "PPR's Vision and Mission," PPR.com. (now is kering.com), accessed March 24, 2014, http:// http://www.kering.com/

en/group/about-kering.

19. "French Group PPR 2012 Sales Rise 20.8 Percent," The Big Story, accessed March 24, 2014, http://bigstory.ap.org/ article/french-group-ppr-2012-sales-rise-208-percent.

20. Steve Siler,"Fiat 500 by Gucci - Auto Shows," Car and Driver, accessed March 24, 2014, http://www.caranddriver.com/ news/fiat-500-by-gucci-at-the-geneva-auto-show-news.

21. Deborah Arthurs, "24-hour Queue... Sold Out in 30 Minutes" Mail On-line. accessed March 24, 2014, http://www. dailymail.co.uk/femail/article-2062599/Versace-H-M-collection-Donatella-greets-desperate-shoppers-website-crashes.html#ixzz2MpMNLM2x.

22. Kamelia Angelova, "Jason Wu's Target Collection Sells Out In One Morning," Business Insider, accessed March 24, 2014, http://www.businessinsider.com/jason-wus-target-collection-sells-out-in-one-morning-2012-2.

23. Ikusmer Observatorio del Comercio, "Luxury Goods Worldwide Market Study." Finance, 11:43:33 UTC, accessed March 24, 2014, http://www.slideshare.net/Ikusmer/ luxury-goods-worldwide-market-study?qid=3bc31fd1-b0f6-4cba-89df-6ce2f8e155f3&v=qf1&b=&from_search=2.

24. Ibid.

25. "Vertu," Vertu Official Website, n.d. http://www.vertu.com/.

26. Bose Corporation History - The 1990's and Beyond,"Funding Universe, accessed March 24, 2014.http://www.bose. com/.

27. Susanna Kim, (August 20, 2012). "Apple (AAPL) Becomes History's Most Valuable Firm on iPhone 5 Rumors". ABC News. ABC News Network. Retrieved August 20, 2012.

28. "2012 Apple Form 10-K," October 31, 2012, accessed March 24, 2014, http://investor.apple.com/SECFilingNav. cfm?FilingID=1193125-12-444068&CIK=.

29. L. Schiffman and Lazar Kanuk L., Consumer Behavior,(New Jersey: Pearson Prentice Hall Publishing, 2009),84-87.

30. Wells and Prensky,Consumer behavior, John Wiley and Sons, New-York,1996.

31. Ian Phau, Marishka Sequeira, and Steve Dix, "Consumers' willingness to Knowingly Purchase Counterfeit Products," Direct Marketing: An International Journal, 3,no.4(2009): 262 - 281.

32. John U. Farley and Donald R. Lehmann, "Cross-National 'Laws' and Differences in Market Response" Management Science, 40,no.1 (1994):111,122.

33. G.Hofstede and J-C Usunier, "Hofstede's Dimensions of Culture and Their Influence on International Business Negotiations," in International Business Negotians, edited by Ghauri Pervez, Usunier Jean-Claude, (Amesterdam: Pergamon; 1999).

34. "Disillusioned Hedonist Shoppers," The Economist, February 11, 2014. http://www.economist.com/blogs/ schumpeter/2014/02/luxury-goods-market.

35. Kapferer, Jean-noël, Strategic Brand Management, (Great Britain: Kogan Page, 1997.),87-89.

36. J.L. Nueno and J.A. Quelch, "The Mass Marketing of Luxury," Business Horizons, 41, no.6, (2008):61-8.

37. "The Five Species of Luxury Consumer," WSJ Blogs - The Wealth Report, December 21, 2010, accessed March 24,

2014 http://blogs.wsj.com/wealth/2010/12/21/the-five-species-of-luxury-consumer/.

38. "The 5 Types of New Affluent Consumers," American Spa, accessed March 31, 2014, http://www.americanspa.com/spa-business/5-types-new-affluent-consumers.

39. "Talkin' 'Bout My Label," *The Sydney Morning Herald*, accessed March 31, 2014, http://www.smh.com.au/lifestyle/diet-and-fitness/talkin-bout-my-label-20110720-1ho7s.html.

40. Ibid.

41. "Unity Marketing's Luxury Report 2012," Unity Marketing, accessed March 24,2014, http://www.unitymarketingonline.com/cms/Home/Luxury_Press_Releases/5-25-2012_Luxury_Report_2012.php.

42. "Luxury Market Trends in Emerging Markets - An Overview by Athena Tavoulari," Stanton Chase International's Executive Newswire, accessed March 31, 2014, http://executivenewswire.stantonchase.com/2012/01/luxury-market-trends-in-emerging-markets-an-overview-by-athena-tavoulari/.

43. Glyn Atwal and Alistair Williams, "Luxury Brand Marketing", *Journal of Brand Management*, 16,no.5/6(2009):338.

44. Manfred Krafft and Murali K. Mantrala, *Retailing in the 21st Century - Current and Future Trends*, (Berlin: Springer,2010), 206.

Chapter 3

INTO THE

HUNDRED BILLION DOLLAR BUSINESS
– Chinese Luxury Market Overview

More and more global luxury companies have long realized that they will need China's growth to power their own in the next decade. But to keep pace, they will also need to understand the external contributors of the Chinese luxury market—economic, societal, and technological changes—that are shaping it and their customers' behavior: "This is not an easy task—not only because of the fast pace of growth and subsequent changes being wrought on the Chinese way of life, but also because there are vast economic and social dynamic differences across China." This chapter will focus on the power of Chinese luxury market, its consumers and the trends that lead to the future.

THE EXTERNAL CONTRIBUTORS OF THE CHINESE LUXURY MARKET
GROWING ECONOMIC STATUS – AN HISTORIC TURNING POINT

Between 2000 and 2010, the economy in China tripled in size, surpassing Japan to become the second largest in the world after the United States. Research undertaken by McKinsey[2] suggests that, "barring major world economic shocks, China's GDP will indeed continue to grow, at an annual rate of some 7.9 percent over the next ten years compared with 2.8 percent in the United States and 1.7 percent in Germany. The difference is that China's growth is driven by consumption - It will account for 43 percent of total GDP growth by 2020, compared with a forecast contribution from investment of 38 percent."[3] This research also suggests that by 2020, Chinese GDP will contribute 19 percent of world economic output, compared with 9 percent in the year 2010, which will surpass that of the United States.

In addition, the expansion of China's economy will continue, especially through its 14 burgeoning cities, which appear on the list of the world's top 25 cities in terms of absolute GDP growth for the next decade.

By 2020, the GDP of some clusters of cities will be similar to that of some current developed markets. The GDP of the Chengdu cluster—a region of 29 cities in western China—will equal that of Austria in 2010, while the GDP of the Shandong by land cluster will equal South Korea's present GDP. By 2020, GDP growth in Shandong will match that of Belgium.[4]

CHANGING SOCIAL DYNAMICS THAT INFLUENCE CONSUMPTION BEHAVIOR

Behind the economic performance in the Chinese market, there are many social dynamic factors influencing shopping behavior:

• Continuous rapid urbanization influences shopping channels

The current rate of urbanization is likely to continue. It is reported "by 2020, some 850 million people, representing about 60 percent of the total population, will be living in urban areas, up from about 650 million in 2010. Around 20 percent of these 850 million will be first-generation migrants from rural areas."[5]

The process of urbanization fuels the growth of the consumer market by widening the afford-ability and availability of goods that will also influence luxury in-store shopping, making it more accessible to a wider range of consumers.

• Improvement of social security to ensure the shopping environment

Concerns in China about how to pay for health care and retirement have thus far accounted for high personal savings. The Chinese government is planning to extend social security by, for example, increasing the coverage of retirement pensions in urban areas by 40 percent, from 250 million people to 350 million by 2015.[6] Following this plan, continued industrial and financial reform could increase investment-related sources of income, which people will be more likely to spend on consumption of luxury goods.

• Improvement of the E-commerce market environment encourages on-line luxury shopping

Following the new laws and rules in Internet e-commerce regulations, the Chinese government is working on improving the environment and the security level of on-line shopping. With the development of second and third tier cites, on-line shopping will be more important for residents to gain knowledge and ownership of luxury goods.

THE GROWTH OF MARKETING IN SOCIAL MEDIA

China, as the most populated country in the world, with over 1.3 billion inhabitants, also maintains the world's second largest economy and is expected to become the largest by 2016.

China has more than 560 million Internet users; as brands ramp up marketing efforts in China, they are increasingly prioritizing digital channels focusing on social media.[7] Because the Chinese government blocks many Google properties, including YouTube, Blogspot, and Google+, along with Facebook and Twitter, Chinese users spend their time on Chinese propertied sites such as Kaixin, Douban, and Jiepang.

CIC has just released a refreshed China social media landscape info-graphic for 2014 [figure 10 on following page]. It shows that more players have emerged in the country's social media space, especially the 'Mobile Social,' which features mobile-only social networks like WeChat, Guanxi, and Momo.[8]

Among all these social sites, there are three headed for competition: WeChat (Chinese Tango), Sina Weibo

(Chinese Twitter) and Taobao (Chinese E-Bay). During the 2012 Olympic Games opening ceremony, Twitter recorded almost 10 million related mentions. Sina Weibo, on the other hand, had 119 million. In the year of 2012,

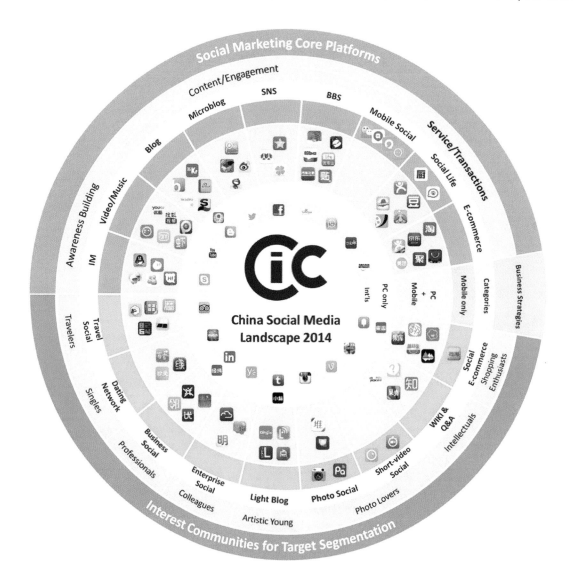

Figure 10 CIC Chinese Social Media Landscape

WeChat was hitting multiple overseas markets, accumulating more than 300 million users. The biggest day in the history of US e-commerce was Cyber Monday 2012, with an estimated record $1.5 billion in sales across on-line retailers in a single day. Last year, Taobao doubled that on Singles Day[9] (11/11), seeing $3.06 billion in sales.[10] By looking at the large scale of Chinese social media and websites, we see a huge potential for brands to develop their social media marketing strategies to gain awareness, even with marketing shares taking place on the Internet.

THE OVERVIEW OF CHINESE LUXURY MARKET
THE GROWTH OF CHINESE LUXURY MARKET IN 2012

46BILLION SALES IN LUXURY GOODS IN 2012

Chinese consumers spent about 46 billion U.S. dollars on luxury goods in 2012, with 27.1 billion U.S. dollars spent abroad and 18.9 billion U.S. dollars at home, according to data recently released by U.S. investment banking firm Goldman Sachs.[11]

It is reported that the Asian economy (except Japan) will gain a full recovery in 2013 and the growth rate will reach 6.9 percent. China's economic growth will amount to 8.1 percent, which will further help the sale of luxury goods, and total consumption of luxury goods in China is expected to top 30 billion U.S. dollars in 2015.

SOME LESSONS MARKETERS LEARNED IN 2012

Red Luxury's website announced an article named "Chinese Luxury Market: Lessons Learned In 2012" discussing the new trends in the Chinese luxury market in 2012.[12]

1. Made for China Only

Chinese customers want to be surprised. Touches of Chinese traditions in branding or product design have higher possibility of winning consumers.

2. The Future is Mobile

With over a billion smart-phone users, China is the world's largest mobile market with a substantial 81 percent year-over-year growth compared to just 5 percent growth experienced in the U.S., according to Catalyst.

3. Navigate China's Digital Landscape

Understanding culture differences is not enough to win in the Chinese market. Luxury marketers have to navigate China's digital landscape with different key players and where western digital marketing strategies often do not apply.

4. Manage Social Media

China is home to the world's most socially active on-line population. 95 percent of Internet users in Tier One, Two and Three cities are registered on at least one social media site and more than half use micro-blogs. Nearly all of the luxury brands have a social media presence in China.

THE DIFFERENT DEFINITIONS OF LUXURY IN CHINA

DIFFERENT CONTENT OF LUXURY ACROSS CULTURES

Luxury derives from the Latin word "luxus", which means "the indulgence of senses, regardless of cost."[13]

An undoubted element of extravagance is involved, but in the Western culture, "Luxury" is more or less neutral and free of criticism, actual or implied. On the other hand, in China, the word "Luxury" consists of two characters, which put together form a word indicating extravagant and wasteful use of wealth.[14] Therefore, in China, the word luxury has a negative connotation. The reason for this is that, throughout China's history, the social morals of Confucianism, Taoism, and Buddhism have taught that life should have no recklessness, no arrogance, and no showing off.

Not only emperors throughout Chinese history but also the Chinese government nowadays have encouraged the virtue of frugality, making luxury consumption with its negative connotations conflicting for the Chinese to engage in.[15] Moreover, in 2005 the Chinese government introduced the "Socialist Concept of Honor and Disgrace" to promote "modern socialist values."[16] The interesting point here in the luxury context is, – "It is advocated to know plain living and hard struggle; do not indulge in luxuries and pleasures.[17]

Accordingly, luxury consumption is still referred to as something negative from the government's point of view.

However, the rapid growth of the Chinese luxury market (China being the second largest luxury market in the world) shows that Chinese consumers to a high extent do not live according to the "modern socialist values" which were promoted by the government.[18]

WHAT THE WORD "LUXURY GOODS" – "奢侈品" MEANS TO THE MODERN CHINESE

Chinese customers' understanding of luxury is still at a preliminary level, and some misunderstanding may also exist. In China, instead of directly naming goods as "luxurious brands," Chinese consumers typically use neutral nouns such as "expensive brands","top brands" and "big brands." All these obscure names could only lead customers' cognition of luxuries into further confusion.[19] The Chinese word for "Luxury" has two characters. It shows the basic attitude of Chinese people towards to the luxury goods. The first one "奢"(Chi) means "more than actually needed," and the second one "侈"(She) means "people possess more than ample things pending for use." Together as a word, the two Chinese characters mean luxury or luxurious. Therefore, the Chinese definition of luxury has an obvious derogatory sense, extended as "squander and excessive pleasure seeking".[20] It has to be emphasized that in Chinese culture there is a definition of luxurious but not for luxury goods. "Luxury goods," written in Chinese as "奢侈品", is an imported word.[21] And the "奢侈" by itself also refers to a luxurious lifestyle.

MAJOR PLAYERS

PERFORMANCES OF THE "BIG THREES" IN CHINA

A report by LVMH, PPR, and RICHMONT – luxury's biggest three conglomerates – paints a far less pessimistic picture. Both PPR and LVMH reported strong first-half profit growth, driven by sales in 'hard' luxury goods such as watches and jewelry, whilst Richemont confirmed a sales increase of 24 percent for four months ending at July 2012.[22]

LVMH

LVMH, which by far is the largest luxury corporation in the world, reported a rise in first-half revenue in 2012 by 12 percent to €12.97 billion, driven by selective retailing's strong growth and the Wines and Spirits Division's out-standing sale performance; meanwhile, the recurring operations increased profit by 20 percent.

However, the Fashion and Leather goods Division only had a rise of ten percent, which includes brands like Louis Vuitton, Givenchy and Celine. LVMH noted that marketing costs had pulled down the margin of Louis Vuitton but they remained confident that the brand's profits would recover in the second half. [23]

RICHMONT

In May 2012, the world's second largest luxury goods group, Compagnie Fianciere Richemont, posted record sales and profits for fiscal year 2012: "Overall sales increased by 29 percent year-on-year to €8,867 million, while the company's profit increased by 43 percent to €1,540 million, attributed in part to aggressive retail expansion in Mainland China and the re-invigoration of boutiques in Europe and China." [24]

In July 2012, Richemont announced that operating and net profits increased by between 20 percent and 40 percent in the first half of 2012 as sales surged. The Swiss maker of IWC watches and Cartier jewelry said trading for the four months ending in June 2012 showed sales rising 24 percent on a reported basis from a year earlier.

PPR

"PPR delivered a highly satisfactory performance in the first half of 2012," noted chairman and CEO François-Henri Pinault, going on to report revenue growth of 17 percent in a "lackluster economic climate." The Luxury and Sport & Lifestyle Divisions' revenue increased more than 25 percent, "propelled by the sales momentum of all Luxury brands, across all regions."[25]

PPR's luxury division profit growth was up 30 percent for the first half year of 2012, with profits at Yves Saint Laurent rising more than threefold and profits at Bottega Veneta up 58 percent. "We are confident that we will be able to continue growing our revenue in the second half of 2012 and that our full-year financial performance will outstrip that of 2011," expressed CEO Francois-Henri Pinault in a statement.[26]

BEST BRANDING PRACTICE IN CHINA

Up on the strong growth in average income, nouveau riche and a deep culture heritage of gift giving for different occasions, the rise of the Chinese luxury industry came as no surprise.[27] Despite the higher selling prices in domestic China, the luxury industry continues to expand with new foreign luxury brands entering the competition.

Brands who start to see the potential of the Chinese luxury market will stop struggling in other parts of the world.[28] It is very important for the luxury brands to balance the much-protected "exclusivity" of brand image for luxury goods while brands continue to expand and grow in the Chinese luxury market.

In the digital age, how brands perform in the virtual community is also an important factor in building up one's brand equity. An analysis of the "performance of luxury brands on-line activities"[29] uses presence scores to measure whether or not a particular luxury brand is mentioned in the communities. According to the rank, Louis Vuitton is the number one on the list with 76 percent of luxury and fashion communities discussing the brand. Number two is Hermes with 75 percent and Chanel comes in third with 74 percent. Here are four brands picked as having the best branding and promotion practices in the Chinese luxury market:

1. Louis Vuitton: Deepen brand knowledge and transcend brand culture through acclaimed platforms

In June 2011, Louis Vuitton showcased its brand legacy with "Louis-Vuitton Voyages" at The National Museum of China.[30] The practice of using exhibitions to enhance brand knowledge is not new, but the location for Louis Vuitton is quite unique. Louis Vuitton is the first commercial brand the museum agreed to partner with for exhibition. The symbol and status associated with acclaimed platforms such as The National Museum of China could be transferred to brands. By having an exhibition in The National Museum of China, the brand wishes to show that it is not simply a luxury brand, but rather its deep cultural heritage and history is praiseworthy; the cultural connotation of luxury brands are therefore magnified. This practice was also followed by BVLGARI with its "125 Years of Italian Magnificence" exhibition in The National Museum of China and Chanel's "Culture Chanel" exhibition in The National Art Museum of China.

2. Gucci: Leveraging on Chinese elements to draw connections with consumers

In April 2012, Gucci appointed Li Bing Bing[31] as the new face and brand ambassador for its Asia-Pacific market. Li will be the new Gucci woman and featured in Gucci's advertising campaign in Mainland China, Hong Kong and Taiwan. Gucci later showcased its focus of the Chinese market by having a first-ever fashion show in China in April 2011. In 2011, Gucci opened 12 new stores in mainland China with plans to open 10 more in 2012, among which over half are in second and third tier cities. For luxury brands, leveraging its rich foreign history and using foreign models for campaigns have been the norm in China. However, as the Chinese market matures and brands start to move into Second and Third Tier cities, using Chinese elements in one's branding initiatives might be more effective. Some companies may not choose to adopt a Chinese brand ambassador directly, but will seek to relate to the Chinese customers by using Chinese models on their runways or inviting Chinese celebrities to sit in the front row seats of runway shows.

3. Chanel: Mastering brand storytelling to anchor brand knowledge

Classics and icons are important for luxury brands. The legendary story of Chanel's founder Gabrielle "Coco" Chanel is quite well known in Europe; in China, her story is just starting to show its magic, which will bring a big effort for developing the awareness of the brand in the immediate future. Leveraging the iconic Mademoiselle Chanel has always been a key branding strategy for Chanel. True "storytelling" goes beyond simply using Coco Chanel's name or image in advertisements and promotion, especially in China. In 2011, Chanel organized an exhibition titled "Culture Chanel" in Shanghai and Beijing.[32] The effect goes beyond simply introducing Coco Chanel. In China, the home of a multitude of brands, having storytelling in the branding "tool kit" is a necessity to anchor the brand's esteem and knowledge. Chinese consumer's capacity to perceive and differentiate brand codes is still in a maturation stage. Therefore, brand messages combined with storytelling will be highly advantageous, especially for foreign luxury brands.

4. Burberry: Step out of comfort zone to leverage digital strategy for differentiation

Social media, especially in China, has been a tricky platform for luxury brands due to the fear for lack of control. While some choose to stay rather cautious and conservative, Burberry successfully differentiated itself by integrating diverse social media channels and Chinese shopping habits into its digital strategy. As a start, Burberry has official accounts on five different top social media platforms in China. In April 2011, Burberry then surprised viewers with an innovative 3D hologram runway show in Beijing that was streamed live on its official pages to generate buzz and praise. Burberry's digital strategy goes beyond social media; its e-commerce website is also differentiated by incorporating unique features which are tailored to Chinese shoppers. With over 513 million Chinese Internet users and growing, there is a big potential for luxury brands to build their own strong e-commerce platform to sustain future growth in this sector.

EMERGING CONTEMPORARY DESIGNER BRANDS AND THEIR ACTIVITIES IN CHINA

With more Chinese luxury consumers in Shanghai and Beijing moving beyond logo-heavy brands and towards less ostentatious niche brands, contemporary designer brands become their new love. Brands such as Alexander McQueen, Maison Martin Margiela, Miu Miu, Stella McCartney, and Alexander Wang are heavy on quality and contemporary design style, which brings refreshing ideas of design and rareness of ownership. While second and third tier cities recently celebrated the opening of their first Louis Vuitton stores, over the past year Beijing welcomed brands that are less well known (or counterfeited) in mainland China, but popular elsewhere in Asia as well as Europe and North America. These brands have steadily found new fans among the more fashionable Beijingers.[33]

The contemporary designer brands market them as the "unique and true" luxury brands that are not commonly recognized but those who understand luxury brands and have better taste should know and buy these brands. In addition to these brands, interest is growing among a certain subset of Chinese luxury lovers for brands such as Céline, Chloé and Lanvin. These brands probably won't compete with LV, Chanel or Gucci directly, but they'll definitely continue to grow and gain marketing share in China in the future.

THE ACCESSIBLE LUXURY BRANDS IN CHINA

With China's expanding middle class and an increasing younger luxury consumer group, a new product niche market—accessible luxury—is growing fast. Also known as "mass" or "affordable" luxury, these affordable luxury brands occupy the middle of the price spectrum between generic brands such as Gap, Zara, Levis and high-end luxury brands, such as Louis Vuitton, Chanel, and Gucci.[34] These brands offer consumers well-known brand names and promise quality without burning holes in their pockets. Their prices vary depending on the brand and the product category. But in general, jewelry usually costs 800 – 8000RMB ($127 – $1270) per piece, and hand bags are priced between 1500 – 8000RMB ($240 – $1270) each.

Affordable luxury brands mainly appeal to the young and the middle class. As an example:

> Wang Qian, a 27-year-old fresh graduate says that Folli Follie is her favorite brand. 'The price is just right, the designs are trendy and the quality is good,' explains Wang. This is the exact image affordable luxury

brands try to achieve.[35]

This gives an example of how the accessible luxury brands serve the consumers with a 'glimpse' of the luxury lifestyle experience with affordable price points. Like Folli Follie, many brands market themselves exclusively within the affordable niche market in China. A few examples include Coach, Michael Kors, DKNY, and Calvin Klein. On the other hand, many high-end luxury brands have accessible sub-brands catered to the same target market but in a high price range, such as See by Chloe, Armani Exchange by Giorgio Armani, and MCQ by Alexander McQueen.

The most successful accessible luxury brand in China since its entry to the market in 2003 has been Coach, which — despite making a significant proportion of its items in China — has maintained a strong reputation in the country, particularly among the Entry-level-luxury consumers in Second and Third Tier cities.[36] In 2012, Coach opened about 30 stores in China, and more than half of them are in the Mainland. Since buying back its retail businesses in Hong Kong, Macau and Mainland China in 2008 and 2009, Coach has seen sales climb rapidly, from $108 million in 2010 to $188 million in 2011. In 2012, the company was shooting for sales of "at least" $300 million. By 2014, Coach expects China to be its leading market.[37]

CONSUMER ELECTRONICS - THE NEW LUXURY PRODUCTS FOR CHINESE PEOPLE

1. Apple

Apple has been an iconic brand for as long as consumers have been buying technology. It has built up an army of fans in China who are fiercely protective of the brand.[38] Outlets in China selling the iPhone rose to 17,000 in the period that ended December 29, from 7,000 a year earlier. That helped Apple boost sales in the Greater China region to $6.83 billion in 2012, from $4.08 billion a year earlier.[39]

The reason behind the increasing purchases of Apple products actually shows consumers' thirst for luxury goods: "In 2009, for instance, Chinese customers snapped up nearly a third of the luxury goods sold in the United Kingdom and 60 percent of luxury products sold in France."[40]

As for Apple, many ordinary Chinese consumers obviously consider its products a luxury item although whether the price tag of the iPhone at about 5000RMB (about $800) is steep enough to be considered a luxury item is debatable. Consumers believe that an iPhone is the least expensive purchase that can bring them closer to experiencing high society and a luxurious lifestyle, and is also the most cost-effective in terms of satisfying vanity.[41]

2. Vertu

Different from Apple's iPhone, Vertu—a former unit of Finland's Nokia OYJ—has come up with a niche cell phone with swanky features to help customers stand out from crowds of more plebeian phones with a luxurious style and well-designed functions.

Vertu is marketed as a luxury product in the global cell phone market. The products of Vertu are retailing for up to $300,000 with fine calf leather, alligator skin or diamonds and are sought-after status symbols among the wealthy elite in Asian countries, especially China. In China, the world's largest mobile phone market, the market size for luxury phones alone is expected to grow to 1.64 billion RMB in 2017, up nearly 60 percent from 1.05 billion RMB in 2012.[42]

THE OVERVIEW OF LUXURY CONSUMERS

China has become the second largest market of luxury products with an annual increase of more than 30 percent in 2010. Moreover, China will become the largest market of luxury goods in the immediate future, which makes in-depth research of luxury consumption in China important to all the luxury companies. Existing research[43] conducted indicates a number of typical Chinese cultural values and motives of luxury consumption in China. According to the research, there are also several types of customer segmentations of Chinese luxury consumers.

STUDY OF VALUE AND MOTIVES OF LUXURY CONSUMPTION IN CHINA

VALUE SYSTEM OF CHINESE CONSUMERS

Nowadays, the Chinese luxury consumer's value system can be seen as three parts: the traditional Chinese value system, the socialist Chinese value system, and the Western value system.

• The Traditional Chinese Value System

From the 1980s to 2010, social wealth rapidly increased with around 10% of growth average each year. The Mainland Chinese consumer became increasingly wealthy with better financial opportunities. It became a trend to openly display individual success—the luxury goods and designer brands effectively communicated this status and wealth. However, the overall core of this phenomenon is "the honest pursuit of better living conditions."[44] Better living conditions translated into higher quality products and upscale brands. This is the reason why luxury brands perfectly fulfill the needs of Chinese consumers from all angles—cultural, social, and economic—thereby attributing to a more modern, powerful, and self-confident approach to life.

• The Socialist Chinese Value System

After the implementation of the Open Policy by Deng Xiaoping, the updated Chinese socialist values were refined as modernity, wealth, achievement and success. Therefore, financial and career success and achievements naturally became a way for people to distinguish themselves from others.[45]

In the luxury consumption of Mainland China, it is common to see a person carrying an authentic Louis Vuitton bag while riding a crowded, public bus or subway in the downtown area. The basic cause of the increasing consumption of luxury products results from the socialist value system – by following along with the market-driven economy, consumers inherently retain the idea of equality. Based on the steady development of economics and increasing consumer confidence towards the future's potential, Mainland Chinese luxury consumers believe that they are, in essence, the same as each other. Even if they cannot afford a luxury product today, they will save up several months to buy it in the near future.[46]

• The Western Value System

As the Western countries represent advanced technology, super powers and modern values, the Chinese seek to pursue these values the best they can.[47] This is the reason why Western values can be said to have a strong influence on the Chinese consumer value system.

Personal liberty, post-modernism, as well as modernity, achievement and success are the attributes that influence Chinese society. Luxury consumption is one of the fields that reflect these influences and efforts.

Overall, the 21st century value system of the Chinese luxury consumer is a "veritable melting pot"; strong values of modernity, wealth and success are dominant. The three attributes in the value system will be the core power behind changing consumption behavior and overall marketing performance of luxury brands.

MOTIVES OF LUXURY CONSUMPTION IN CHINA

"Go to China" is now the slogan for most of the luxury companies in the world. "Chinese Luxury" is now getting more attention because of the dynamics of the Chinese luxury consumer value system as well as the motivation of consumption, which is different with the West.[48] The emerging Chinese luxury market bounds with unique characteristics: "more vanity oriented than taste; buying beyond afford-ability not to lose face; younger, between 20 and 40; favoring products but experience; preferring popular foreign brands and overt logos; mainly for gift giving etc."[49] Most of the Chinese luxury consumers desire "conspicuous consumption before fully realizing basic needs."[50] However, there are also affluent consumers in China who are becoming more rational, seeking experience and brands' heritage more than symbolic value.[51] The "Rarity Principle"[52] suggests that "if everyone owns a particular brand, prestige is eroded and thus the luxury component is taken away."[53] There is much research studying different relationships among brand awareness, purchases and dream value in the Chinese

To show personal taste	21%	To express own unique personality and taste through the consumption of luxury brands and differentiate themselves from others.
To highlight status	21%	To show their wealth, identity and status and prove they are not ordinary people.
To ensure the quality of life	19%	To associate the stability and reliability with the high quality of luxury brands.
To use luxury as a lubricant	21%	To use luxury as a lubricant for their social and personal networks.
To release self	18%	To pursue the change of their life and release them from the pressure of a career.

Figure 11 Motivation of Luxury Consumption from Unicview's Research

luxury market. The scale of luxury consumption motivations, developed by following guidelines suggested by Dr. Churchill,[54] includes 22 items on three dimensions:

• Personal Motivation, expressing unique taste and individualism

• Quality Motivation, seeking high quality

• Social Motivation, conforming oneself to the society

Recent research[55] done by Unic-View shows that there are five primary motivations for Chinese women's consumption of luxury brands. [see figure 11]

As figure 12 shows, another research done by KPMG[56] in 2008, 2010 and 2011 shows that connoisseurship and self-awarding are two strong motivators of Chinese luxury consumption. The strongest motivation is self-awarding with over 40 percent of the interviewee saying they purchase luxury products "to pamper themselves" or "to enjoy the luxury experience" in the research of 2011.

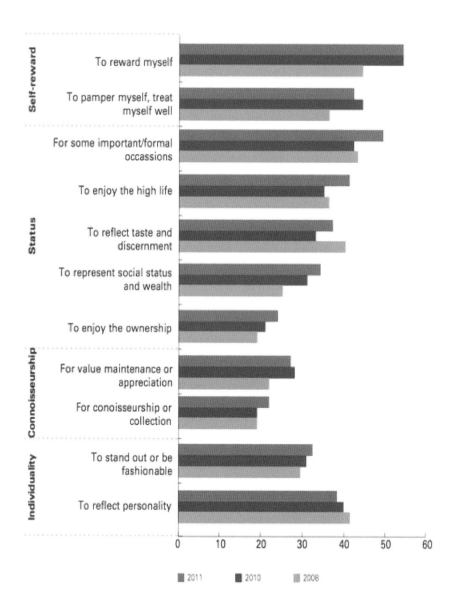

Figure 12 Motivation of Luxury Consumption in China

STUDY OF CHINESE LUXURY CONSUMER SEGMENTATION

The Mainland Chinese luxury market is unique and complex enough to require multi-criteria methods for analysis in order to understand its variety of aspects, such as geographic, demographic, and psycho-graphic aspects.[57]

Geographically, the regional differences in Mainland China are varied; in China, there are mainly four large regions: North, South, East and West. Within the regions, there are different provinces with thousands of cities. Cities then can be further classified into tiered cities according to the city's size, area, as well as level of economic development.

Demographically, the segmenting elements classify Chinese luxury consumers into traditional groups. Demographic segmentation is used by dividing the consumer into groups based on variables such as age, gender, income level, education, occupation, etc. Demographic segmentation is one of the most popular segmentations for customer study and marketing research.

Psycho-graphically, these segments in the luxury market have been defined as four groups known as "luxury lovers, luxury followers, luxury intellectuals and luxury laggards with three dimensions according to the different psycho-graphic aspects: collectivism-individualism, analytical-impulsive thinking, conspicuous-functionality for luxury goods"[58] as shown in figure 13.

	North (Beijing)	East (Shanghai)	South (Guangzhou)	West (Chengdu)
Lovers	15.6%	13%	22.5%	3.3%
Followers	15.6%	26.1%	27.5%	33.3%
Intellectuals	42.2%	33.7%	30%	16.7%
Laggards	26.6%	27.2%	20%	46.7%

Figure 13 Physiographic Segmentation of Luxury Consumer in China

Considered together with geographic segmentation, and according to the research of Lu,[59] figure 14 below shows the distribution of the psychographics in different regions of China. According to the results, the segmentation shows the concentration of luxury lovers and followers, representing 31.2 percent of the total market in first tier cities. They are the pioneers who purchase new products and who are often defined by the media as opinion leaders and the influencer of the luxury market in Mainland China. On the other hand, intellectuals and laggards focus more on functionality and individualism.[60]

Here are some of the significances shown in this system:

1) The pursuit of ancient China's luxurious lifestyle influences the Chinese luxury consumption behavior today. There is a need for international luxury brands with a distinguished lifestyle; moreover, there is also a need for Chinese original luxury brands to continue the legend. 2) Chinese traditions encourage people to lead a benign but not an extravagant lifestyle. Instead, frugality and discreetness are the proper ways to lead life and are deeply rooted in the core social value system in China. Therefore, frugality and discreetness are being encouraged in both the traditional and social value systems in "comparison to modernity, wealth and achievement values, which were confirmed twice by socialist and western value systems."[61]

As a result, the psychological values in Chinese society are conflicted. This conflict is influenced in the attitudes

	Dimension 1: Conspicuousness / Functionality	Dimension 2: Individualism / Collectivism	Dimension 3: Impulsive / Analytical thinking
Lovers	Conspicuousness	Collectivism	Analytical
Followers	Conspicuousness	Collectivism	Impulsive
Intellectuals	Functionality	Individualism	Analytical
Laggards	Functionality	Individualism	Impulsive

Figure 14 Segmentation Across with Geographic

and behaviors of luxury consumers in China. Additionally, with the trends in the Chinese luxury market toward the future, the decisions that international luxury companies need to make are filled with challenges and unpredictable efforts to their future marketing performance in the Chinese luxury market.

STUDY OF SHOPPING TRENDS IN CHINESE LUXURY MARKET
OVERSEAS VS DOMESTIC

The most important trend of the Chinese luxury market now is the increasing shopping habits of Chinese tourists. Sage Brennan of China Luxury Advisers points out that "Chinese tourists are on track to take more than 155 million overseas trips by 2020, and will make 1.7 million arrivals in the United States in 2013."[62]

An article in the *China Time*, pointed out that between January. 20 and February. 20, Chinese consumers spent $4.3 billion on luxury watches, leather goods, fashion goods and perfumes in Europe, which amounted to 65 percent of the total sales of luxury goods in the market during this period. Over the same period of time, Chinese luxury goods buyers spent nearly $2 billion in Hong Kong, Macau and Taiwan, which was equivalent to 87 percent of the total luxury goods sales in those markets. However, the number of people willing to purchase high-end items in Mainland China decreased significantly, amounting to only 10 percent of their spending overseas at $830 million. The figure declined by $920 million, or 53 percent, to a five-year low from the spending on luxury goods in 2012, recording at $1.75 billion.[63]

In the past five years, luxury companies have been acquiring as many stores in China as possible, from first tier cites to second then third tier due to the perspective of the fast growing Chinese luxury market. The 2012 annual report of LVMH, KERING (previously PPR), and McKinsey's recent research[64] suggests that sales made of Chinese consumers overseas continue to grow faster than sales in domestic China. According to the research from BCG, "only one third of sales to consumers are made in Mainland China. Two thirds are made abroad, including Hong Kong, Macau, and Europe."[65]

It seems like the luxury stores in Mainland China are now becoming a point of reference. Customers "do research," such as getting to know the price and color options, trying on products in the domestic stores then making purchasing while they are traveling. The BCG research also shows that prices are the main reason behind luxury shopping overseas. Around 93 percent of the participating luxury customers considered it more advantageous to buy goods overseas than in domestic stores. Around 85 percent agreed the number of collections and designs of luxury products available abroad were higher than the domestic market, and 65 percent considered the goods they bought overseas less likely to be counterfeit.[66]

With this trend happening in luxury shopping, plus the government control in luxury gift giving to political officers, it is a challenging time for all the luxury brands who own stores and have business with China.

IN-STORE VS ON-LINE

Digital media plays an increasingly important role in China; KPMG's survey[67] shows that about 70 percent of potential luxury customers search for information for luxury brands or products on the Internet at least once a month. It also suggests a surge in on-line shopping intentions, with 40 percent of respondents indicating they are interested in making luxury purchases on-line, which has increased from 22 percent in 2011.[68]

According to the research[69] by China E-Commence Research Center, there are four things about the on-line luxury shopping trend luxury companies need to know:[70]

1. ABOUT 80 PERCENT OF CHINESE LUXURY CONSUMERS NOW WILLING TO BUY ON-LINE

Research shows that 62.7 percent of respondents with experience shopping on-line said that they felt luxury goods are "suitable to buy on-line," with 57.4 percent of consumers with the intention of shopping on-line soon agreeing. In total, 85.4 percent of respondents expressed a willingness to buy luxury goods on-line, while the remaining 14.6 percent said that they aren't yet prepared to try it out.

2. SECOND-TIER CITIES HAVE THE MOST POTENTIAL

The choice is a critical factor motivating consumers in smaller Second and Third Tier cities, where many brands have yet to expand in China. There is 28.4 percent of respondents said that e-commerce is the only way for them to purchase certain luxury goods, with the vast majority of these individuals living in Second and Third Tier cities.

3. WOMEN GO FOR CLOTHING & COSMETICS, WHILE MEN GO FOR WATCHES

Consumers in China aren't just becoming more diverse in terms of which brands they buy; they're becoming more diverse in terms of what products they're buying. The study identified that female respondents are more inclined to purchase luxury apparel, footwear, handbags, cosmetics and fragrances than male respondents, who mainly shopped on-line for electronics, watches and jewelry.

4. QUALITY ASSURANCE, AUTHENTICITY ARE CRITICAL

Perhaps the most obvious finding of the survey is that the vast majority (76.9 percent) of consumers feel quality assurance and product authenticity are the most important factors driving them to make a luxury purchase. Additional factors noted by respondents included better pricing than brick-and-mortar stores, the credibility of the website itself, secure transactions and after-sales service.

According to Bain & Company's report,[71] China's e-commerce sales are expected to reach 1.5 trillion in the next three years and may overtake the U.S. as the world's largest e-commerce market with on-line sales growing to represent 7 percent of all retail sales.[72] As on-line luxury shopping is becoming a main trend, many luxury retailers and brands such as Neiman Marcus and Coach have launched Chinese e-commerce sites and more brands are expanding their business through e-commerce.

THE GROWING POWER OF YOUNGER CONSUMERS IN LUXURY CONSUMPTION

More and more younger Chinese people are becoming fans of luxury goods, increasingly making up the share of Mainland China's luxury consumption. Reported by the World Luxury Association (WLA), "On average, Chinese luxury consumers are 15 years younger than their European counterparts and 25 years younger than their U.S. counterparts."[73] This research also suggests that the minimum age of China's luxury consumers has dropped to 25 in 2010 from 35 in 2007. Its recent report shows that "73 percent of Chinese luxury consumers are under the age of 45 years old, and 45 percent of Chinese luxury consumers are between 18 to 34 years old. This ratio in Japan and Britain are 37 percent and 28 percent respectively."[74] Finally, it predicts that the luxury consumer aged between 25 and 30 will become the dominant group of luxury consumption in China in the next three to five years.[75] Second, to be able to predict future luxury shopping trends and market growth's direction in Mainland China is to truly understand this younger consumer group from multiple perspectives. Lastly, the younger consumers that the researchers above referred to are exactly covered by the subject of this thesis – the China One. Today, they are the younger consumers, and tomorrow they will have the mainstream consumption power of the Chinese luxury market. This is the key, and also the core, of this study's goal. The following parts of this thesis will closely examine the facts and answer those questions through the primary and secondary research of the China One.

NOTES

1.   "Meet the Chinese Consumer of 2020 | McKinsey & Company," accessed March 31, 2014, http://www.mckinsey.com/insights/asia-pacific/meet_the_chinese_consumer_of_2020.

2.   The latest survey, "Meet the 2020 Chinese Consumer" carried out in 2011, gauged Chinese consumers' attitudes and spending behavior in relation to about 60 types of products and 300 brands. The respondents represented a wide range of incomes, ages, regions, and cities. They accounted for 74 percent of China's total GDP and for 47 percent of the total population.

3.   "Meet the Chinese Consumer of 2020 | McKinsey & Company," accessed March 31, 2014, http://www.mckinsey.com/insights/asia-pacific/meet_the_chinese_consumer_of_2020.

4.   Ibid.

5.   "Communiqué of the National Bureau of Statistics of People's Republic of China on Major Figures of the 2010 Population Census (No. 1)". National Bureau of Statistics of China. April 28, 2011, accessed March 31, 2014, http://www.stats.gov.cn/english/NewsEvents/201104/t20110428_26449.html.

6.   "Meet the Chinese Consumer of 2020 | McKinsey & Company," accessed March 31, 2014, http://www.mckinsey.com/insights/asia-pacific/meet_the_chinese_consumer_of_2020.

7.   "Understanding China's Digital and Social Media Landscape," Experience Management Blog, accessed March 31, 2014, http://www.sprinklr.com/social-scale-blog/china-digital-social/.

8.   Willis Wee, "China's Social Media Landscape 2013 (INFOGRAPHIC)," Tech in Asia, April 2, 2013, http://www.techinasia.com/china-social-media-landscape-2013/.

9.   In China, people refer to Nov. 11th as the Single Day because the date is written as four "1"s which represents the four people standing alone.

10. "Understanding China's Digital and Social Media Landscape," Experience Management Blog, accessed March 31, 2014, http://www.sprinklr.com/social-scale-blog/china-digital-social/.

11. "China's Luxury Consumption Hits $46 Billion," accessed March 31, 2014, http://english.peopledaily.com.cn/90778/8093172.html.

12. "Chinese Luxury Market: Lessons Learned in 2012," Red Luxury, accessed March 31, 2014, http://red-luxury.com/brands-retail/chinese-luxury-market-lessons-learned-in-2012.

13. Pierre Xiao Lu, *Elite China: Luxury Consumer Behavior in China*. (Hoboken,NJ: John Wiley & Sons,2008), 155.

14. Ibid.

15. Ibid.

16. Ibid.

17. Ibid.

18. Ibid.

19. "The Dawn of the Luxuries in China," NR Tiger Website, accessed March 31, 2014, http://www.ne-tiger.com/en/Design3-03.html,2011.

20. Ibid.

21. Ibid.

22. Joe Fox, "Luxury's Big 3 Resilient to Economic Slowdown," Best Italian Leather Blog, accessed March 31, 2014, http://blog.bestitalianleather.com/fashion/luxurys-big-3-resilient-economic-slowdown/.

23. "LVMH 2012 Annual Report", accessed March 31, 2014, http://www.lvmh.com/uploads/assets/Com-fi/Documents/en/Press_release_PDF/LVMHAnnualResults2012_VA.pdf, 2012.

24. "Richmont 2012 Annual Report", accessed March 31, 2014, http://www.richemont.com/images/investor_relations/reports/annual_report/2012.pdf.

25. Fox.

26. Ibid.

27. "The Best Practices of the Digital Marketing for Luxury in China," Marketing China, accessed March 31, 2014, http://marketingtochina.com/digital-marketing-for-the-luxury-in-china/.

28. Ibid.

29. Ibid.

30. The exhibition featured 4 showrooms which celebrated Louis Vuitton's 157 years of history and presented luggage and bags that demonstrated the brand's evolution. The National Museum of China is highly regarded by Chinese citizens to be one of the best museums which display top tier art pieces that contributed to culture changes in China.

31. Li Bing Bing is a superstar in China known for her poised beauty and global recognition in *Snow Flower and the Secret Fan* and *Resident Evil: Retribution*.

32. The exhibition was "specially made for China" and aimed to further introduce Coco and what inspired her to create classics such as the interlocking C symbol, No.5 perfume, the camellia flower along with concepts such as "invisibility," "hidden luxury" and more. The purpose is to establish an emotional connection with potential customers and transcend the association between Chanel's signature designs (aesthetic symbols) with the iconic Mademoiselle Chanel (story).

33. Jing Daily, "With Tastes Changing, Understated Luxury Stands To Gain In China," accessed March 31, 2014, http://www.jingdaily.com/with-tastes-changing-understated-luxury-stands-to-gain-in-china/18788/.

34. Pocket says, "The Affordable Luxury Opportunity in China," Red Luxury, accessed March 31, 2014, http://red-luxury.com/

brands-retail/affordable-luxury-opportunity-in-china.

35. Ibid.

36. Ibid.

37. Jing Daily, "Accessible Luxury Brands Ride China's Middle-Class Wave," accessed March 31, 2014, http://jingdaily.com/bridge-brands-target-chinas-budget-constrained-fashion-obsessed/21427/.

38. "Luxury Brand Mobile Use Must Shift from Marketing to Experience: Vibes Exec - Luxury Daily - Mobile," accessed April 4, 2014, http://www.luxurydaily.com/luxury-brand-mobile-use-must-shift-from-marketing-to-experience-vibes-exec/.

39. Bloomberg News, "Apple China Revenue Jumps 67% as Sales Outlets Double," Bloomberg, January 23, 2013, http://www.bloomberg.com/news/2013-01-24/apple-china-revenue-jumps-67-as-sales-outlets-double.html.

40. Ibid.

41. "Why Are Chinese Consumers Crazy for Apple?," INSEAD Knowledge, accessed April 4, 2014, http://knowledge.insead.edu/world/china/why-are-chinese-consumers-crazy-for-apple-559.

42. "Vertu Targets China's Rich with Its Android-powered Luxury Phones," NDTV Gadgets, accessed March 31, 2014, http://gadgets.ndtv.com/mobiles/news/vertu-targets-chinas-rich-with-its-android-powered-luxury-phones-337095.

43. "The European Business Review » Management New » Luxury Consumer Behavior in Mainland China: What Exists Behind the Facade of New Wealth?," accessed March 31, 2014, http://www.europeanbusinessreview.com/?p=2418.

44. Lu, 178.

45. Ibid.

46. Ibid.

47. Ibid.

48. Tom Doctoroff, *Billions: Selling to the New Chinese Consumer*, (Martin Sorrell, Palgrave MacMillan, 2005),205.

49. Yiping Song and Baijun Zhu, "Behind Fever: Patterns and Motives of 'Chinese Luxury'", *European Advances in Consumer Research* (Volume 8), 2010:47.

50. N.Y. Wong, and A.C. Ahuvia, "Personal Taste and Family Face: Luxury Consumption in Confucian and Western Societies," *Psychology & Marketing*, 15,NO.5(1998): 423.

51. Ibid.

52. Bernard Dubois and Claire Paternault,"Observations: Understanding the World of International Luxury Brands: The 'Dream Formula'," *Journal of Advertising Research*, 35,NO.4(1995): 69-76. Mason, R. M., Conspicuous Consumption–A Study of Exceptional Consumer Behavior, Grower Publishing Company,1981.

53. Ibid.

54. G.A. Churchill, "A Paradigm for Developing Better Measures of Marketing Constructs," *Journal of Marketing Research*, 16,NO.1(1979):63-73.

55. Uniview, *Exploring Motives of Luxury 2013 Brand Consumption in China*, 1st issues, 2013, accessed March 31, 2014, http://www.unicview.com.cn/webmanage/uploadpic/2013131392251609571.pdf.

56. "Luxury Experience in China, KPMG," 2011, accessed May 17 2013, http://www.kpmg.com/FR/fr/IssuesAndInsights/ArticlesPublications/Documents/Luxury-experiences-in-china-2011.pdf.

57. Pierre Xiao Lu,"Luxury Consumer Behavior in Mainland China: What Exists behind the Facade of New Wealth?" *European Business Review,* (Sept.10ct.2010):53-56.

58. Pierre Xiao Lu, *Elite China: Luxury Consumer Behavior in China,* (Hoboken,NJ:Chichester: John Wiley, 2008),235.

59. Ibid.

60. Ibid.

61. Ibid.

62. "A Critical Question for Luxury Brands: What Do Chinese Tourists Want?" 2013, Jing Daily: The Business of Luxury and Culture in China, accessed May 17, 2013, http://www.jingdaily.com/a-critical-question-for-luxury-brands-what-do-chinese-tourists-want/26182/.

63. "Chinese Luxury Shoppers Spend a Fortune Avoiding Domestic Market," *Want China Times,* accessed May 17, 2013, http://www.wantchinatimes.com/news-subclass-cnt.aspx?id=20130224000095&cid=1102.

64. "Luxury Without Borders: China's New Class of Shoppers Take on the World", McKinsey, Dec. 2012 http://www.mckinseychina.com/wp-content/uploads/2012/12/the-mckinsey-chinese-luxury-consumer-survey-2012-12.pdf.

65. "Slowdown in China's Domestic Luxury Market," 2013, accessed May 14 2013, http://fashionbi.com/newspaper/slowdown-in-china-s-domestic-luxury-market.

66. Ibid.

67. "Global Reach of China Luxury | KPMG | CN," accessed May 17, 2013, http://www.kpmg.com/cn/en/issuesandinsights/articlespublications/pages/global-reach-china-luxury-201301.aspx.

68. "Chinese Luxury Consumers Are Increasingly Purchasing Overs | KPMG | GLOBAL," accessed May 17, 2013,http://www.kpmg.com/global/en/issuesandinsights/articlespublications/press-releases/pages/chinese-luxury-consumers-purchasing-overseas.aspx.

69. "Four Things to Know about China's Luxury E-Commerce Market," *Jing Daily: The Business of Luxury and Culture in China,* accessed May 15,2013, http://www.jingdaily.com/what-you-need-to-know-about-chinas-luxury-e-commerce-market/19872/.

70. China E-Commerce Research Center released a survey of 1,762 potential on-line luxury shoppers in 100 cities throughout China — roughly divided in terms of gender, with 897 male and 865 female respondents — that addressed that very question and identified some very interesting trends in the Chinese high-end e-commerce market.

71. Serge Hoffmann, Bruno Lannes, and Jessica Dai, "China E-commerce: Heading Toward RMB 1.5 Trillion," accessed May 17, 2013, http://www.bain.com/Images/BAIN_BRIEF_China_e-commerce.pdf.

72. "Chinese Luxury Market: Lessons Learned in 2012," Red Luxury, accessed March 31, 2014, http://red-luxury.com/brands-retail/chinese-luxury-market-lessons-learned-in-2012.

73. "2010- 2011 World Luxury Association Annual Report", accessed May 17, 2013, http://www.worldluxuryassociation.org/.

74. "Why Are Chinese Luxury Consumers Relatively Young?" Peopledaily.com. accessed May 17, 2013, http://english.peopledaily.com.cn/90778/7913841.html.

75. "China's Luxury Consumers Younger Than World Average," *People's Daily On-line.* accessed May 17, 2013, http://english.people.com.cn/90001/90778/90862/7399847.html.

Chapter 4

MEET THE "CHINA ONE"
– From the 'Little Emperors' to the 'New Chinese'

With the development of the Chinese luxury market, a new mainstream customer group is catching marketers' attention all over the world – The China One group. As an unique generation grown up with traditional eastern education and western lifestyle, China Ones have become the most important consumer toward luxury shopping. In order to understand their shopping behavior, this chapter will introduce the China Ones' basic information, historical background as well as case studies toward their values.

WHO ARE THE "CHINA ONE"?
DEFINITION OF CHINA ONE

China One is the name that I created for the generation whose members were born between 1980 to 1989 (known as Post 80s) in Mainland China. This generation currently ranges in age from 23 to 33 and constitutes about 216.9 million which makes up a major portion of China's young adult demographic nowadays.

Calling this group of people China One relates to the idea that first, the members of this group are the first generation in China after the introduction of the One-Child Policy which lead their lifestyle and family values to differentiate from earlier generations; second, they are the first generation born after China's economic reform in the late 1970s, which makes the social environment different from the earlier generation. Additionally, compared with the younger generation, the Post 90s and 00s, the China Ones are in the beginning of their careers and starting to have more purchasing power. They are the key of today's Chinese market and also the future.

THE ORIGINAL CONCEPT OF CHINA ONE

China One's original concept is the "Post 80s". The Post 80s (八零后) are a unique generation of today's Chinese society, a group of 200 million people. A young Chinese writer, Xiaobing Gong, first used the concept "Post 80s" in order to refer to the group of young writers who were born between 1980 and 1989. The Post 80s are "growing up in a relatively stable and affluent society characterized by economic boosting, material prosperity, and cultural diversity."[1] They are seen as a demographic group that "serves as a bridge between the closed, xenophobic China of the Mao years and the globalized economic powerhouse that it is becoming."[2]

In order to emphasize the uniqueness of the one-child characteristics and the group's geographic location – China – the China One is often used to replace the concept of Post 80s. They are a hybrid generation whose status requires more than their year of birth. It is a group of young people with tradition and modernity, combining Eastern thought and Western culture with distinctive characteristics and differentiating them from previous generations.

HISTORICAL BACKGROUND OF CHINA ONE

THE ONE-CHILD POLICY

According to the report by the Chinese Population Control Department, the earth's population is increased by 160 people each minute.[3] China is home to more than 20 percent of the total population in the world which makes it play an important role in helping the stabilization of world population growth. In order to alleviate the social, economic and environmental problems caused by population issues, the Chinese Government introduced the "Family Planning Policy" in 1979, which is better known as the "One-Child Policy."

The One-Child Policy (officially translated as "Family Planning Policy") restricts urban couples to only one child, while allowing additional children in some cases; this includes twins, rural couples, ethnic minorities, and couples who are both only children themselves.

Under the One-Child Policy, as the first generation of the only child in the family by law, the China One have faced many new situations, such as influences from western culture, in addition to having been given more purchasing power in the families as they grow to young adults.

THE CHINESE ECONOMIC REFORM

The Chinese economic reform (simplified Chinese: 改革开放政策; literally "Reform and Opening Up Policy")," refers to the program of economic reforms called 'Socialism with Chinese Characteristics' in the People's Republic of China (PRC) that was started in December 1978 by reformists within the Communist Party of China (CPC) led by Deng Xiaoping.'"[4] With the effort of the Chinese economic reform from 1978 to 2010, "unprecedented growth occurred with the economy increasing by 9.5 percent a year."[5] At present, China's economy has become the second largest in the world and is projected to surpass the US and become the largest economy by 2025.[6]

The success of China's economic reform and the manner of its implementation has made many changes in Chinese society. With the income increasing, people are looking for a new lifestyle which mixes Chinese traditional values with western culture's influence. The China One is the generation that grew up during this time period. They had much more access to western culture – they are the generation reading Chinese textbooks and drinking Coca-Cola while watching Japanese cartoons. Higher household incomes gave them the possibility to explore their interests in different fields as well as to gain a better education.[7]

THE "LITTLE EMPEROR" IN THE "4-2-1 FAMILY"

The "4-2-1" Family refers to the collapse of the traditional large Chinese family scale into the "four grandparents and two parents doting on one child".[8] The Little Emperors of the One-Child policy have changed the traditional family beyond recognition: "in the past, the power in a household emanated from the father."[9] Now the family structure is totally centered around the only child in the family, which shifted from earlier structures that supported "the culture of filial piety" and which has caused much concern in Chinese society.[10] Living and growing up within the "4-2-1" Family, the China Ones have a better childhood and education, making them consider themselves the lucky generation who have the main purchasing power and are the decision makers.

The "Little Emperor" Syndrome (or Little Emperor Effect) is an aspect of China's One-Child Policy where the only children in the family (including both boys and girls) gain seemingly excessive amounts of attention from their parents and even their grandparents. Combined with the increased purchasing power within the family and parents' desire of giving anything they could to make their child's life better and easier, the phenomenon is considered to be problematic.[11] China Ones know they can always get something, even if their parents cannot afford, because of the extra support from their grandparents. The adults in the family are giving all they can to fulfill the need of their one child. This is the reason why "The Little Emperor" is the title given to the China One group in their childhood period – including both boys and girls. In conclusion, this phenomenon is the unique family structure built by the One-Child Policy – the "4-2-1" Family.

WHAT THE "CHINA ONE" DOES AND HOW THEY THINK

Growing up within this significant time period, the 250 million China Ones are the first generation to walk through the new era of market reforms and opening up of China's economy. With the full attention of the "4-2-1" Family, the China One are introduced the "notion of personal luxury and imported individualism from abroad"[12] to define their own behavior characteristics toward their hybrid value system.

UNIQUE CHARACTERISTICS OF THE CHINA ONE

Through the Chinese Lens – Two Ways of Seeing the World

Researchers at MIT point out that Westerners and East Asians exhibit different neurological patterns when making judgments about the same scenarios.[13] The key difference is the recognition of individualism; easterners focus more on a group's value and interest, whereas westerners concentrate more on finding individual identity.

Following with the country's modernization and developing economy, Chinese people started to explore the world in a different way. The trend of globalized communication and the mix of eastern and western value systems influence the China Ones who grew up with open minds. They start to focus more and more on their free minds as individuals. This changing perspective drives their changing behavior. For the China Ones, they are on a journey of exploring the world; even more so, they are also on the way to exploring themselves.

Super Spending Power by Redefining the Basic Needs

With their parents earning more and no sibling competition, the China Ones have more spending power than other generations could imagine. Their needs are the drivers of the whole family in the majority of cases, which propels the China One to become an important spending power to push the economy forward.[14]

In the family, the China Ones started with a higher quality of life by their eager-to –please parents. Throughout their childhood, they have redefined the concept of "Basic Needs." Beyond basic needs of food and clothing, they want certain brands and items to feel "equal" to their peers.

The China Marketing Research Group estimated that the spending by China Ones contributes to more than 20 percent of the country's total spending. According to their research, the average monthly expense for raising a China One is around 39 percent to 52 percent of the household total expenses.[15] Moreover, the total cost of raising a China One from birth to high school graduation is an average of about 490,000 RMB, but many families spend more than 1 million.[16] As the China Ones grow, they are able to experiment with the shopping experience as a way of personal expression and identity building. They are shopping based on a new need, the need beyond the basic needs – the social and identity need.[17]

The Tight Connection with the Internet

Growing up in a media-filled, high technology - dominated, and brand focused world, the China One's generation is better educated and are more technically literate than the previous generations in China.

The China Ones equip themselves with laptops, smart phones, video games and all the applications in these high tech devices to connect with Internet and social media. As a China One, the Internet is not only a necessary communication tool but also the significant difference for this generation.[18]

As the sole heir, the China Ones grow up under a great deal of pressure, competing with peers and working long hours with little time for themselves. They must be successful in their career and personal lives to payback all the support and attention gained throughout their childhood. Living in a digitally oriented world without siblings, the Internet became their 24/7 friend who helps them take a break and socialize with other China Ones. With the build up of on-line activities, the Internet has become the channel of communication and socialization as well as education. China Ones explore and exchange the latest news and information with each other on-line. They choose what to read, what to listen to and what to believe.

CASE STUDIES OF CHINA ONE'S VALUE AND LIFE STYLE

CASE I: A STORY OF LALA'S PROMOTION – CHINA ONES' WISHFUL WHITE-COLLAR LIFESTYLE

With rising salaries and a new social mobility, the China Ones imagined an exciting future built on good careers and social status. They are eager to don western-style suits, gossip with coworkers about office politics and dream about being a manager or entrepreneur someday – the so-called "White Collar Lifestyle." This desire is not only self-motivated, but also influenced by the China Ones' family values – to have a good career and salary to make their parents proud, to make their friends impressed. There is a best-selling book named *A Story of Lala's Promotion*,[19] written by Li Ke, which describes a story of how a young professional girl is promoted in her position. It became very popular because it is actually a "How To" guide towards how to live and work as a white-collar worker.[20]

When the movie version was released in 2010, it featured an elevated consumption storyline within the main plot. The movie upped the ante of products from normal lines to high-end products. The products from luxury brands that were placed in the movie attracted lots of attention and showed a strong influence on increasing sales. The product placement in the movie made a great success because it brought strong connections with China Ones - their lifestyle and value standards.

CASE II: A SONG NAMED "OLD BOYS" – CHINA ONES' COMMEMORATED DREAM AND REAL LIFE

As many China Ones appear to be mainstream, their internal worlds are more multidimensional than is assumed. "This trend of between crafting and external appearance to meet societal expectations while holding a more intimate personality inside"[21] is a hallmark of the China Ones. The themes of the movie are the dilemma between dream and reality, personal and family, and how China Ones often sign for the sacrifices they made to survive tough competitions. They have hidden the dream inside of their hearts and do what they have to do to lead their lives.

A film named *Old Boy*[22] tells a story of two school friends who once dreamt about becoming superstars like Michael Jackson. As they grew up, they abandoned their childhood dream for real life – one became a barber, one became a wedding emcee. Life felt average until they got a chance to go to a TV talent show and rekindle their dreams. The ending of the story is they didn't win. However, when the China One audiences watched, they tear up because of the emotional connection that the movie made to their own life experience; the never ending pursuit of their dream. Born in a unique time period of Chinese history, China Ones are holding traditional values about memories and friendships from the traditional Chinese culture; meanwhile, the globalized cultural boom also challenges them. When these two elements somehow encounter each other, it brings a huge emotional reaction from the group, how they see themselves and how things inspire them to keep their dreams alive.

CASE III: CHINA ONE'S IDENTITY THROUGH CONSUMPTION PREFERENCES

With many China Ones appearing to be mainstream, their internal worlds are more multidimensional than is assumed. For brands who are looking to target the China Ones, it is challenging to make the right marketing strategic decisions. "Li Ning," a domestic athletic brand, has made a successful demonstration in the past five years. In 2008, Li Ning changed their tag-lines from "Anything is Possible" to "Make the Change" which implemented its renewed marketing strategy – to encourage the China Ones, who are the target customers, to change their life and the world. The ethos was made with new advertisement prints and medias. The company made a statement that they are domestic brand; unlike Nike and Adidas, it needs more support from China

CHINA ONE, THE LOVE OF THE LUXE

Ones to compete with global brands. After this promotion strategy had been pushed to the market, it helped Li Ning greatly increase sales as well as the awareness in Hong Kong and Taiwan. This case shows that the key of marketing to China Ones is to understand their value standards and the unique sense of responsibility held by the generation. This marketing campaign clearly fits the self-identity that China Ones had greatly influenced their product choices for Li Ning.

NOTE

1. Simon Elegant, "China's Me Generation: China's Me Generation," Time, accessed March 31, 2014, http://content.time.com/time/magazine/article/0,9171,1675626,00.html.

2. Ibid.

3. "Family Planning in China", Information Office of the State Council of the People's Republic of China, accessed May 17, 2013, http://www.china-un.ch/eng/bjzl/t176938.html.

4. Angus Maddison, Contours of the World Economy, 1–2030 AD. Essays in Macro-Economic History, (Oxford: Oxford University Press,2007),382.

5. "Liberalization in Reverse," The Heritage Foundation. accessed May 21,2013. http://www.heritage.org/research/commentary/2009/05/liberalization-in-reverse.

6. Ibid.

7. Ibid.

8. Ibid.

9. "Young Chinese Couples Face Pressure from '4-2-1' Family Structure," People's Daily On-line. accessed May 17, 2013,http://english.people.com.cn/90001/90782/7117246.html.

10. Louise Branson, "China's Brat Pack; Generation of Only-children," Sunday Times (London, England) 19 June 1988, accessed May 17, 2013.

11. Andrew Marshall, "Little Emperors," The Times (London, England) 29 Nov. 1997: 44.

12. Bergstrom, Mary. 2012. All Eyes East: Lessons from the Front Lines of Marketing to China's Youth. Macmillan.

13. Richard Nisbett, The Geography of Thought: How Asians and Westerners Think Differently...and Why (New York: Free Press,2004),188.

14. Ibid.

15. Xu Anqi, "The Economic Cost of a Child: Changes and Optimization During the Transforming Period," Youth Studies, 12 (2004): 1-9

16. Ibid.

17. Bergstrom, 155.

18. Rebecca Huntley, The World According to Y: Inside the New Adult Generation. (Crows Nest,Australia: Allen and Unwin,2006),102.

19. Li Ke, Du La La Sheng Zhi Ji [A story of Lala's Promotion], (Shaanxi: Shaanxi Normal University Press, 2007),98.

20. Ibid.

21. Bergstrom, 190.

22. Old Boys (Chinese: 老男孩) is a Chinese short comedy film directed by Xiao Yang. It became popular via the Internet. A drama adaption of the film has been announced recently in 2013.

Chapter 5

ALL EYES ON CHINA ONES
– Primary Research of China Ones' Luxury Shopping Behavior

Who they are, how they value things, what they do, where they shop, what they shop and how they shop... The answers to these questions about China One's luxury consumption behavior will lead us to see the future of the Chinese luxury market. Here is a spotlight on them, the new mainstream luxury consuming power in China – All eyes on China One!

OVERVIEW OF PRIMARY RESEARCH
OBJECTIVE

Because the China One group has limited existing direct studies, the objective of the primary research is to truly understand the current shopping behaviors of China Ones and the value-based reasons behind them through first-hand data and information. In addition, in order to further compile the research results into practical recommendations, the information of the current luxury brands' strategies toward China One is needed as well.

EXPECTED RESULTS

During the primacy research, the expected results were:

1. There is little research that directly applies to the China One group; most of the existing studies are targeting the younger luxury consumer in general. The primary research tools use the same framework, and the results will help to confirm the secondary research or adjust the difference in order to further identify the uniqueness of China One's luxury shopping behavior.

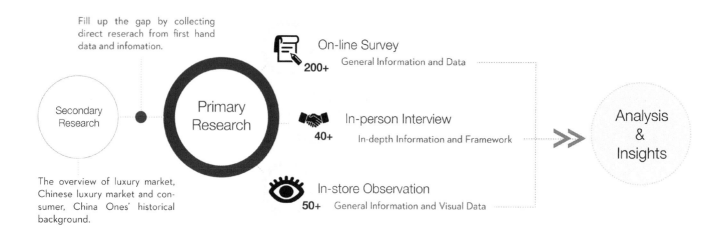

Figure 15 Primary Research Methodologies

2. To build a visualized framework of China One's Luxury shopping behavior and preference: Quantitative research (Survey) will provide numerical data to analyze utilizing statistical results. Also, Qualitative research (Interviews, Observations) will provide in-depth information to help understand China Ones' behavior and the reasons that govern such behavior.

RESEARCH STRATEGY

The primary research strategy chosen for this thesis study is based on the use of a quantitative study and theoretical frameworks, as well as contextual research methodologies. In order to understand China One's luxury shopping behavior towards consuming and interacting with luxury brands through traditional and on-line channels, the following plan of primary research was devised. There are three main methods chosen to fulfill the needs of the primary research: On-line survey, One-on-one interviews, and observation.

As figure 15 shows, since the study required descriptive, explorative and causal insights into the area of China One's luxury consumption values and shopping behavior, the following research design tools were employed to investigate the motivation, study and understand the voice of consumers. Each method is used as a tool to approach the results step by step:

1. Survey: The scope of the survey is to determine, and then better understand, China One's current income status and luxury value as well as shopping behaviors through qualitative data. Due to the limitation of Internet access from the Chinese government, most of the often-used survey channels are not available to target participants in China. Considering the target participants are current young luxury consumers in China, using SOJUMP Survey Services (a Chinese-based platform similar to Survey Monkey) as the on-line survey website can achieve the goal of the research and ensure the quality of the data gained from the questionnaire responses which further leads to valid results. This research was inclusive of both genders of China One, born between 1980 and 1990 throughout Mainland China. Requests to participate were sent by e-mail with the link to the survey. People were also encouraged to pass the link along to others.

2. One-on-one Interviews: The objective of the interview is to examine and identify in-depth, the information needed for developing the China One group's luxury shopping value system. This includes the China One luxury

consuming profile, segmentation, persona study, as well as insights for giving future recommendations to luxury brands to better target the China One group. Due to the limitation of time and resources, the interview section was done within one month, taking place in six cities in Mainland China: Beijing, Shanghai, Shenzhen, Tianjin, Chongqing, and Chengdu. There were 45 interviewees who participated in one-on-one interviews. Each of the participants was given the same six open-ended questions, video recording their reactions and answers. After the interviews were finished, the notes and the videos further generated to gather information and insights that helped with the development of the analysis framework and recommendations.

3. Observation: The objective of the observation is to examine and to identify the current practices and promotion strategies of current luxury brands in the Chinese market in order to determine the opportunities for them to better target and communicate with China Ones. Due to the limitation of time and resources, the observation was done within one month, taking place in 55 stores across six cites. The store visits were done as secret shopping and with pictures taken secretly. The goal for the observation was to determine what are the current in-store and on-line presentations of luxury brands in China; how the luxury brands are communicating with China Ones; and

Section	One Who are the China Ones as luxury consumers?	Two For China Ones, "What are Luxury Goods"?	Three Chinese Luxury Market Current Activities Toward China One
Questions	•Geographic (Urban Cities map, age, gender, occupation...) •Physiographic (habits, 7 types of VALS...) •Unique background as born under one-child policy •Lifestyle Map (time expense, money expense, social networks, technology...)	•What are Luxury Goods? (Price, brand, category...) •What do the luxury goods mean to them? (Why they buy?) •What do they buy? (Money expense, brands, for whom...) •Where do they shop? (city area, retail format, on-line/off-line) •How do they shop? (Technology usage, alone/with others, how often?)	• What are the current communication strategies that luxury brands are having now? • What should luxury brands do to better target and communicate with the China One?

Figure 16 General Question of Primary Research

the potential opportunities for marketing strategies toward China Ones in the future.

RESEARCH QUESTIONS IN GENERAL

The overall questions utilizing the three research methodologies include: China Ones' profile, shopping behavior and Chinese Luxury Market's current strategies toward China One group. Figure 16 has been created to serve as a guide for further development of each research tool.

SURVEY

In order to achieve the objective of the research, the on-line survey is carefully designed to cover the relevant questions. The questions contained dichotomous Yes-and-No questions, multiple choice, as well as questions on a Likert Scale providing the survey data that is needed to obtain the statistics necessary to substantiate the results. The survey sample asked a variety of questions including basic demographic information such as level of education. Other questions ranged from personal opinions about what luxury means to the participants, how they shop for luxury goods, where the information is gathered before shopping, and favorite brands. Figure 17 shows a

Section	Profile and Shopping behavior in general		Attitude toward ownership of luxury goods	Luxury Goods shopping behavior	
Content Included	Participants' basic information, such as name, gender, email, age, city, and occupation. Also provides 5 questions on a 1-5 Liker scale to help participants to define their fashion style.	Participants' financial information, such as monthly income, monthly expenses in general and monthly expenses on fashion related products, as well as luxury goods' expenses.	Participants' definition of luxury goods, the motivation of luxury goods consumption, buying preferences of luxury brands and categories.	Participants' annual expenses in luxury goods, the most recent purchases, the frequency of luxury goods consumption, dream luxury products and future purchasing plans.	Participants' most satisfied luxury shopping experience, how they shop for luxury product, the attitude towards on-line shopping, decision making process and key factors.

Figure 17 Survey Content Design

brief summary of the questions that are included in the survey (See the full version of the survey in appendix B):

SURVEY RESULTS & ANALYSIS

SURVEY RESULTS OVERVIEW

There were 218 valid respondents in the survey sample. As figure 18 in next page shows, the program Microsoft Excel was implemented to compile the data for further analysis.

The results show that about 218 participants come from 30 cities; and about 8 percent of them are the only-child in their families (Who are the China Ones). More than half of the participants are between 26 to 29 years old and have incomes of 3,000RMB and above per month. Most of the participants like on-trend fashion products, which have a mixed casual, relaxing style. Most of them are not loyal to the brands. About 90 percent of the participants have recently purchased luxury goods. Most of their purchases are in apparel, accessories and food categories. They buy luxury goods in order to reward themselves, enjoy their lives as well as show their tastes and self-image. They have strong attitudes toward luxury products and shopping. The most considered attributes of luxury products are quality, design and uniqueness. Most of the participants search for new product information at least one time per month. They love to shop whether by themselves or with friends. Most of the participants have positive attitudes about trying on-line shopping for luxury products, and about half of them have already purchased products through on-line channels.

INDIVIDUAL SURVEY QUESTION RESULTS AND ANALYSIS

Section One: Basic Information and Style towards fashion

This section's five questions are designed to focus on understanding the participants' basic information and their general attitude towards fashion and style. The individual results are shown as follows:

1. Gender and Geographic Location

About 37 percent of participants are male and 63 percent are female. The 218 samples are covered by the first and second tier cities of China and other cities outside these tiers.[1]

About 45 percent of the participants are from the First Tier cities, including Beijing, Shanghai and Guangzhou. About 19 percent of the participants are from the Second Tier cities such as Chongqing, Tianjin, Hangzhou, etc. Around 36 percent of the participants are from other cities in the Mainland China area.

2. Age and China One Identities

About 89 percent of participants are typically the only-child in the family, and so belong to the China One group, the target of the primary research. The participants of this survey are mostly between 26 to 32 years old (about 80 percent of the group).

Most of the China Ones in this age range have finished college and worked for about four or more years. (Chinese students usually go to college at 18 and graduate at 22 years old.) They are the mainstream of luxury product consumption because of their stable income as well as the increasingly mature value and purchasing behavior toward luxury goods.

3. Self-defined Fashion Style

This question was asking the participants to choose a scale between each of the paired-up attributes toward fashion style according to their understanding of their own style and preference.

The favorite attributes are Fashion, Casual, Basic, Relaxing and not strongly Loyal to brands.

These results confirmed the study found from secondary research: China Ones are looking for on-trend, relaxing and simple styles to reflect their taste; they prefer tailored clothes and business styles occasionally for special events, but love casual, relaxed fashion styles for day-to-day wearing. China Ones are not strongly loyal to brands; instead, they love to try different brands and styles to experience the dynamic of fast changing fashion. This result will be further combined with other relevant question results during the in-depth analysis stage.

Section Two: Tell me what you shop?

This section's questions are designed to focus on understanding the participants' basic information towards spending power, buying perception and recent luxury shopping status. The breakdown results and analysis are as follows:

1. Recent Purchasing of Luxury Products in the Past Six Months

About 90 percent of the participants had recently purchased luxury goods. It confirms the secondary research conclusion that the China One group has **great** purchasing power towards luxury goods. Because the percentage of people who have previous luxury shopping experience is fairly high, to find out how the experience was in general became one of the objects for the in-depth one-on-one interviews.

2. Monthly Income VS. Monthly Expenses

About 90 percent of the participants' monthly income level is about 3,000 RMB. The biggest segment within this range is the group "8,000RMB and above." This shows the high-income level within China One group. This suggests the purchases of luxury products remain powerful and will continue to grow in the future as well. About 69 percent of the participants' monthly expenses are between 2,000 RMB and 8,000 RMB. About 10 percent of the participants spend above 8,000RMB per month, which is higher than their incomes.

This supports the secondary research results that some of the China Ones are spending more than they earned by getting support from their parents.

3. Top Three Categories of Monthly Expenses

About 81 percent of them chose "Apparel" as one of the top three expenses. This is showing how important self-appearance is to the China Ones. This group is always staying on-trend, which is also confirmed by the 56 percent rate of people who chose "Accessories." Moreover, the third rated category is "Food"– this is a traditional cultural phenomenon as food is always very important to Chinese people of all ages. After "Food," the fourth is "Rent and Utilities" which was often chosen by the participants who live in the bigger cities for work but do not own an apartment or house yet. Also, there are two categories also highly rated, the "Beauty/Salon/Spa" and "Electronic Products" which more likely have a gender orientation of choice. According to previous secondary research: females tend to spend more in Beauty and Salon; males tend to spend more in Electronic Products.

Section Three: Tell me what you think is luxury? Why do you buy luxury goods?

This section's questions are designed to focus on understanding the participants' value and definition of luxury and the buying motivation behind the behaviors. The results and analysis are listed below:

1. General value of luxury goods in China One group

About 78 percent of the participants chose "Enjoy high quality life." This confirms the secondary results that China Ones are pursuing a high quality lifestyle, and luxury goods are a part of their definition of a high quality of life. The second most popular chosen statement is "Show good taste." This again supports secondary research that Chinese luxury consumers are seeking products to match their taste as a part of their social image. The third most chosen statement is "To feel happy" which is an extension from China One's basic general value system – doing something for the sole reason of being happy. This is a unique value standard, which China Ones hold and developed through their childhood to adult life. "To feel happy" gives China Ones an unbeatable "excuse" to purchase high price luxury products even though they cannot always afford it. They have the ability to ask their parents for money to buy these luxuries so that they can be happy about their uniqueness in their family (the only child) and in the society of modern China. The other two choices have lower rates which are "Prove a successful life" and "To show off" which gives one-sided evidence that China One's luxury shopping motivations are changing from "To buy in order to let others know the ownership" to "To buy in order to satisfy self first." This also shows the luxury purchase behavior of China Ones tend to be more mature.

 2. Value Statement toward Luxury Products

This question shows that there are many positive attitudes toward luxury and purchasing values shown by China Ones. The results confirm the study from secondary research that China Ones are confident in appreciating luxury goods in a mature way – they are focused not only on ownership, but on the brand's connection with them. There are several highlights in this section of questions: First, about 79 percent of the participants agree that the quality of the luxury brands is more important than just the name of the brand itself. Second, about half of the participants believe that the luxury product does not need to be well known; instead, it needs to match with the owner's personality. Third, most of the participants believe that the luxury goods are not only for showing-off, which again confirms the changing perspective of luxury ownership and consumption. In addition, about 20 percent of the participants prefer the experience of luxury products, such as travel, golf or going to a spa. It shows a high interest towards traditional luxury product categories in China One group.

3. Motivation of Luxury Shopping

This is a question designed by KPMG[2] on the research of understanding how the young luxury consumer's shopping motivation leads behavior. The question and the choices are maintained the same for this current study. By doing this, the results can be compared with the research of young luxury consumers in China in general and differentiate the uniqueness that China One has as a smaller group overall.

4. Top Attributes toward Luxury Goods

The top ranked attribute is "Design/Appearance," up to 29 percent of the group. This result shows that design is the most important thing that drives the sales. China Ones tend to find outstanding design and style while they are shopping for luxury goods, which have also been confirmed by secondary research results as well. The second ranked is "Quality/Lasting Longer," up to 22 percent. This shows that the China Ones are considering luxury goods as high quality products at first; some of them are enjoying the high quality of the product as a part of the high quality lifestyle. Besides the top three ranked attributes, the second top-ranked are "Uniqueness" and "Brand Culture/Heritage" which shows that when China Ones are shopping for luxury goods, they want to have something rarely put out to the market; also they tend to shop for the brands that have a long history and culture. On the other hand, there are also some attributes widely considered by western consumers that are not considered by most of the participants such as "Environment friendly," "Brand's social responsibility," and "Celebrities' promotion." This shows the different values that China Ones have as luxury consumers; it also shows that westerners are more developed with shopping decision-making – they care more about the external effort that the luxury goods may have on society.

Section Four: Tell me how you shop for luxury goods?

This section's questions are designed to focus on understanding the participants' luxury shopping behaviors such as how they do research before buying, who they shop together with as well as how the decisions are made. The results and analysis are as follows:

1. Frequency of the Participants Shopping with Luxury Products

About 94 percent of the participants say they shop luxury goods from one time to eight times per year. The most ranked are "2 times" and "3 times." This shows the average purchasing power of the China Ones. Later on, the in-depth interviews will focus on finding out when this shopping happens throughout the year and why.

2.The Top Three Categories of Shopped Luxury Goods and Participants' Favorite Shopping Channels

According to the results, "Bags/Leather Goods," "Watch/Jewelry" and "Shoes" are the top three categories the participants shopped the most, which confirms the general research results of young luxury consumers in China's shopping behavior from the secondary research. As the results show, about 71 percent of the participants prefer to go to brand boutiques to shop. "Mall/Department stores" and "Go Abroad" are the second ranked shopping channels. About 35 percent of the participants also chose "Overseas Purchasing Agency", which is a unique shopping channel adopted by many young people in China in general shopping as well. "On-line Shopping" is the least preferred channel, as about 22 percent of the participants chose it. In the following one-on-one interviews, the reason for the lack interest in on-line shopping will be explained.

3. Luxury Products Information Gathering

The two questions briefly asked about the brief information of how the China Ones do their research and how often they search for the new luxury products. About 41 percent of the participants say they research new product information randomly; also, about 26 percent of them say they search for new products once per month. The following interviews will examine why and how random the information searched is like. The most ranked channel is "See new product through the brands' website." This result confirms the finding from the secondary research: China Ones' lifestyles heavily rely on the Internet. The access to the Internet helps them to keep up with the latest information, which drives the purchasing of luxury products.

4. Shopping Decision-Making Drivers

This question asked about the final decision-making drivers of China Ones' luxury goods purchasing.

Most of the participants (about 79 percent) chose "Match my taste and style," which again confirms that China Ones are looking for luxury products that reflect their image and fit their style. The second ranked is "Limited

Edition/Design." This again shows that China Ones are seeking the uniqueness for themselves through the unique piece of luxury goods they own. The third ranked is "Time limited discount," which shows that promotion and sales really drive the purchase of luxury products. This result also explains the reason why outlets and discount stores are popular among the China Ones—it not only provides a better price for luxury product, but also provides a "must buy" motivation to the China Ones. In the following interviews, the reason and the level of price sensitivity will be defined more clearly.

5. How China Ones Shop for Luxury Goods

About 86 percent of the participants chose to either shop by themselves or shop with friends. This result shows that the China Ones value self and peer opinions more than those of family members. In the secondary research, it is said that China Ones sometimes see the luxury shopping events as social opportunities to further make a gathering with friends after work or during weekends.

6. China Ones' On-line Shopping Status and Potential Opportunities

Only about three percent of the participants say they are not interested in on-line luxury shopping at all; the rest (97 percent) of the participants show an interest toward on-line shopping. Additionally, about 52 percent of the participants say they have done on-line luxury goods shopping before. This result will lead to an in-depth interview with China Ones in order to know the participants' feedback toward previous experience and hesitation of on-line shopping as well as the reasons behind it.

INSIGHT DEVELOPMENT FROM SURVEY RESULTS

After the analysis of survey questions, several highlights occurred: First, China One is a group that has great purchasing power for luxury products. Second, the understanding of luxury goods and the culture are widely developed by China One through self-education and communication with peers. Third, the ownership of luxury goods are no longer the top motivation for China One; instead, seeking individuality, setting trends, as well as a feeling of achievement are China Ones' main motivations for luxury shopping.

1. ATTENTION OF INDIVIDUALITY AND TREND SETTING

Many results from the survey show that China Ones are looking for luxury products that are rarely found and that match their style. They tend to be more creative in expressing their taste through luxury shopping. Identity, image, and uniqueness are what China Ones are looking for. China Ones, as the early adapters, would be the best target for new or niche brands; however, the well-known brands will still take advantage of their purchasing because of the proven high quality and the brands' heritage. Because China Ones are younger than the average luxury consumer, has a higher job status as well as high-education, what China Ones would love to buy and to own will become the trend for the Chinese luxury market.

2. SELF-REWARDING

One of the strongest findings of the survey is that most of the China Ones chose to buy luxury products as a form of self-reward. This suggests that the motivation for spending money is to relieve stress from work, to relax and to enjoy the moment of life. More than 30 percent of the participants search for new luxury products once per month through the Internet, magazines, and from chats with friends. Further improving the experience of purchasing both on-line and in-store will enhance the feeling of achievement to potentially drive the increase of luxury sales of brands.

Overall, the results of the survey show the high level of sophistication of China One's luxury shopping behavior and the emergence of distinct motivations. This can be a sign for brands of how to better serve the China One as an important luxury consumer segment. In the following primary research methods, the reason behind those choices and the deeply hidden value system of China One, will be unveiled, which will further guide the development of recommendations for luxury brands.

INTERVIEWS
INTRODUCTION OF INTERVIEW QUESTIONS AND ANALYSIS PROCESS

SIX GENERAL QUESTIONS OF PRIMARY RESEARCH INTERVIEWS
• How do you define Luxury products/brands?

• Why you buy luxury products?

• What is the one best experience you had when purchasing luxury products?

• What is your dream luxury purchase?

• How do you shop? Who do you shop with?

• Any recent purchases or a plan to purchase?

As the list shows, the interviews were guided by these six main questions. Following the questions, there were relative questions added if the interviewee mentioned any information that is valuable to the research. The added questions varied according to the different responses of the basic questions.

INTERVIEWEES' SELECTION

The 45 participants were selected evenly in gender, 22 males and 23 females [Figure 18 shows a snapshot of some interviewees]. All of the participants were China Ones and confirmed having had previous luxury products shopping experiences. They are located in six cities, which include three First Tier, two Second Tier, and one other city. The interviewees were randomly selected from a sample including 60 people who were recommended by people in my network in China.

Figure 18 China One Interview Participants

INTEVRIEW RESULTS ANALYSIS PROCESS

As the figure 19 shows, the interview analysis process and results development was done within four phases:

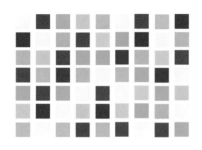

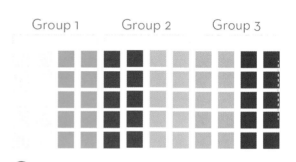

Group 1   Group 2   Group 3

Phase One
FINDING KEY INFO

Starting from going over Interview notes and video clips to generate key ideas of the answers on sticky notes.

Phase Two
COMING-UP GROUPS

Analyzing the content of the sticky notes and starting to come up the general groups of the key words before placing the sticky notes to groups.

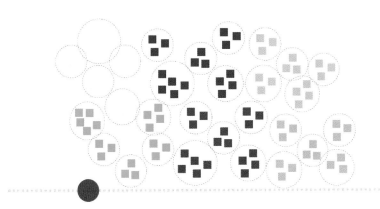
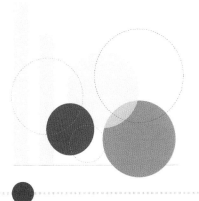

Phase Three
GROUP ANALYSIS
Breaking down to three paired-up groups to further identify connections and opportunities of insights development.

Phase four
INSIGHTS DEVELOPMENT
Combining all the insights in order to develop the framework of China One's luxury shopping behavior and value system map.

Figure 19 Interview Analysis Process and Results Development

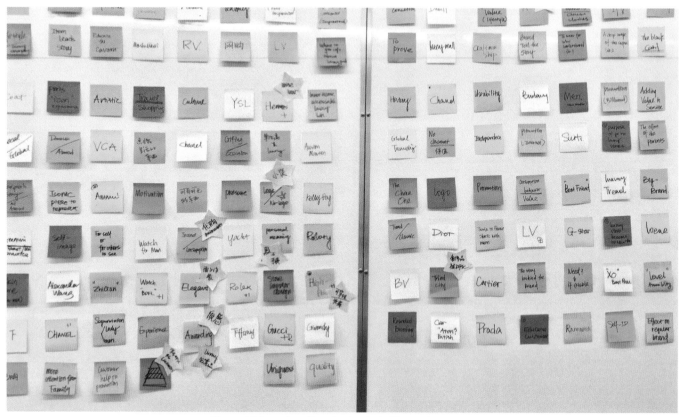

Figure 20 Interview Results Analysis Phase One

Phase One: Information Gathering and Organizing

The interviews of the 45 participants averaged about 30 minutes per person, 20 hours in total. By re-examining the video clips and notes taken during the interviews, there were about 200 sticky notes of information generated from the answers of the questions from the interview.

As figure 20 shows, the sticky notes were placed randomly on a white-board and color-coded to represent different groups of content. Some of the sticky notes contain Chinese characters, which will be translated into English in the in-depth analysis phase.

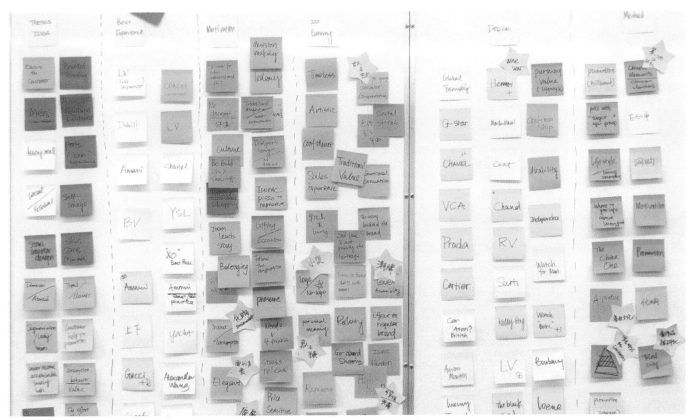

Figure 21 Interview Results Analysis Phase Two

Phase Two: Grouping

According to the objective of this method of primary research, the cohesiveness of the secondary research and primary research findings, the sticky notes were placed within three groups. Each group has two sub-groups, which are strongly connected with one another. Some of the notes could be placed in more than one group. Considering the priorities of the objective, the notes were placed in the most relevant group. As figure 21 shows, the three groups are: group of value (Define Luxury VS. Motivation), group of experience (Best Experience VS. Dream Luxury Products), and group of analysis methods (Ideas for Further Analysis VS. Methods of Analysis).

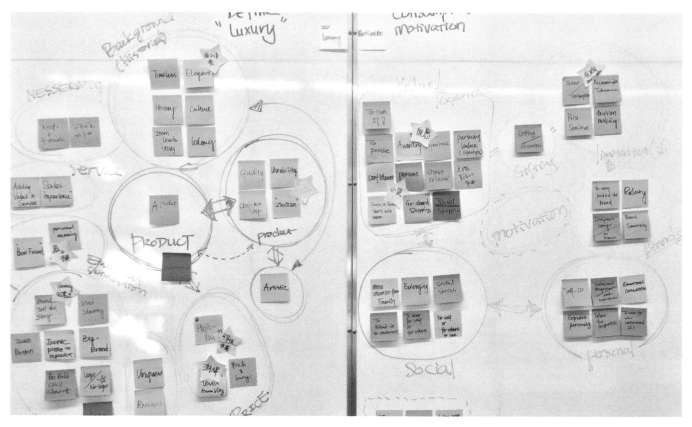

Figure 22 Interview Results Analysis Phase Three

Phase Three: Identify connections and opportunities of insights development in each group

Phase Three takes each group's content to build connections by understanding the context and the true value the notes are representing. Figure 22 shows the process of this stage's analysis. First, the group's notes were individually placed on a white-board. Second, each note was reviewed again to identify the sub-group it belongs to. Third, the notes were placed in small groups with connected notes that have similar meanings. The last step in this phase is drawing the connection lines and the small groups representing meanings. For further insight development, each group's analysis mapping was refined into sketches, then into digital info-graphics.

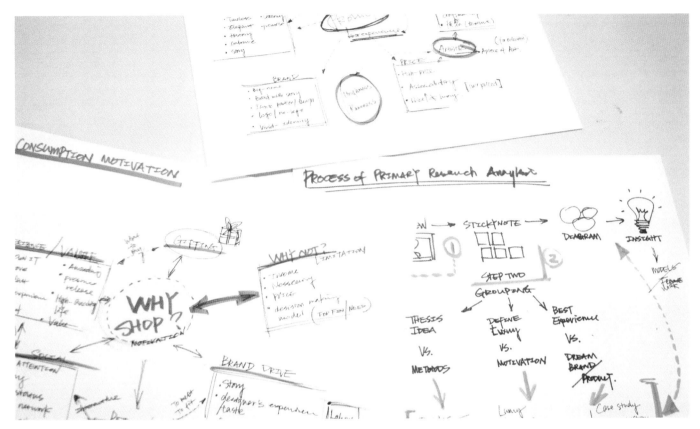

Figure 24 Interview Results Analysis Phase Four

Phase Four: Interpretation of Interview Findings

Phase four is the last step of the interview results analysis and yet the most important step. This phase uses all of the efforts that Phases One through Phase Three have made, combining them with the understanding of this content through the interviews to conduct comprehensible conclusions and insights. What follows are the interpretations of findings from each group of notes with the final info-graphic mapping of results.

INTERVIEW INSIGHTS

1. THE GROUP OF VALUE: DEFINE "LUXURY " VS. MOTIVATION

This group includes the notes that relate to the value of luxury products and consumption preferences of China Ones. As a fundamental basis of the research, this group sets up the core values toward all luxury related values and decision-making. The sub-group of "definition of luxury goods" shows how China Ones see luxury goods as products or even beyond. The sub-group of "luxury purchasing motivation" helps us trace back to the roots of China Ones' shopping behaviors. The outcome of this group will guide the further development of insights and strategy toward China Ones' luxury shopping behavior.

During the research process, about 70 notes were categorized into this group. There were two sub-groups in this category: China One's definition of luxury goods and motivation of luxury goods consumption. What follows are the detailed results for each sub-group analysis.

Sub-Group1-1: Definition of Luxury Goods

After further identification, about 30 notes were categorized in this sub group. After grouping the similar meaning ones together, the connections were drawn out on a white-board. During the secondary research, there were several elements of luxury goods identified as the main attributes for Chinese Consumers in all ages. After understanding each note's meaning and the connections among them all, primary research results of China One's definition of luxury products concludes as follows:

• A luxury good is "a product." This means that luxury goods can be seen as objects that have all the attributes of a product. Luxury products have high quality, outstanding design and maintain better value after purchases. "High quality and high price" are mentioned several times by the China One interviewees. Also, the participants also mentioned "experiential products" such as travel, spas, entertainment, etc. during interviews. This shows the growing maturity the China Ones have towards the understanding of luxury goods.

• During the interviews, most of the participants stated that luxury goods will not be individually considered if there are no brands related with them, which means luxury brands are often combined with the products themselves as a whole when they are the objects referred to as "Luxury Products." One quote from a China One during the interview states, "Luxury goods are representing the legacy of the brand's heritage; without the brand, it is just a product with high quality and a high price." During the interviews, lots of key words were mentioned around brand history and reputation, which shows the high value of the brand image and heritage that the China Ones pay attention to when they are thinking about luxury goods.

• During the interviews, it was determined that China Ones believed that, different from other products, luxury goods may not be necessary for consumers to buy to fulfill their needs; on the other hand, luxury goods may satisfy a want rather then a need. The "want" comes from the unique attributes that luxury goods have: The rareness of the products and the uniqueness they represent with the owner's taste. "It is a piece of art," says one interviewee, while another says, "I appreciate the brands' history and the products' design." The interviewees expressed their focus on the additional value of luxury products, which goes beyond the ordinary attributes the products would carry. This shows how price is considered as one element but not the most important one when China Ones are considering what luxury goods they will buy.

• There were some interviewees discussing the relationship between them and the luxury products they own and use: "For me, it is like a friend of mine, who has the same 'personality'." Another says, "I love it because I can see myself in it." This leads to an interesting finding of how the China Ones are holding emotional connections with the luxury goods they own and use everyday. The emotional connections will be further examined in the following sub-group – Motivation of Luxury Shopping.

Sub-Group1-2: Motivation of Luxury Shopping

After further identification, about 40 notes were categorized in this sub-group. After grouping the related meaning ones together, the connections were drawn out on a white-board.

The secondary research has discussed several motives of luxury goods consumption for Chinese consumers in all ages. Different from luxury consumers in western countries or Chinese luxury consumers in general, China One interviewees showed different ordered motivations of the same attributes/elements during interviews. In other words, while both groups valued an emotional connection, for example, they both ranked them in importance differently. After understanding each note's meaning and the connections among each small group within this category, primary research results of China One's motivation toward luxury products is concluded as follows:

• Most of the interviewees mentioned that they buy luxury goods for themselves because the products fit with their image and taste. It is not about purchasing another thing but the product itself. They see the products as reflecting their self-identification as individuals. Also, they "feel" the products speak for them or that they somehow feel an emotional connection with the products' attributes: quality, design, style, function, etc.

About "质感"

More than five times, the interviewees mentioned they like the "texture(质感)" that the products carried – which in the Chinese language refers to the combination of all attributes that the products carried. During the interviews, some of the participants mentioned that they would still agree that luxury goods need to be practical – even if they are not buying a high priced bag just because they need a bag, they still expect the products to last longer and be practical. Through the interviews, participants said: "Sometime I tend to buy some luxury goods if it is not what I really want or need, if it is a limited edition or has a time-limited discount. I like to pay less for something good also to be unique in the style so that no one has the same one." This shows the price and the style sometimes become the purchasing trigger for China Ones' luxury shopping behavior.

• As discussed in the previous sub-group, luxury goods are always related to brands. The value of luxury goods is ensured by the brand's heritage, reputation and products' design. No matter if the brands are famous or not, the China Ones are always trying to purchase products with the brand they appreciate. "I am a Chanel lady", an interviewee said. "I love Chanel not only as a brand, but also as a value or lifestyle tag-line for me as a girl who is elegant and independent. The brand and the founder of the brand always inspire me to be who I am and to chase after my dreams." During the interviews, when the interviewees talked about why they like certain brands, they always showed a strong connection with the brands they loved. They have a full understanding and knowledge of the brands' history, style and the latest runway shows. Some of the interviewees said they bought some products from luxury brands that are not well known by their peers or family members. One interviewee said: "I bought a pair of Rick Owen's pants. It is just a pair of black casual sweat pants, which has no logos of special significance. I don't expect everyone to recognize the brand. I like the brand." Another one said: "I love Alexander McQueen. I love the brand's ethics and the designer. He is so talented and it was really sad to hear that he passed away a few years ago," an interviewee said when she was talking about the scarf she was wearing during the interview. This is one example that shows how mature China Ones are as luxury consumers, even though they are as young as 24 to 32 years old.

• Most of the China One interviewees discussed the experience related to the motivation of luxury consumption. "I just want to own it. I don't normally used but I love to have it in my closet," as one interviewee mentioned during the interview. Another one said: "I worked really hard for a better career, sometimes, I love to buy luxury goods to reward myself." Also, there was a girl who mentioned: "To buy luxury goods makes me feel confident and relaxed. I love to shop for my boyfriend and myself. It sometimes is like a pressure release for me." All of the comments relate with the shopping experience and the ownership of luxury products that China Ones are buying. Many China One interviewees mentioned in the defining luxury goods question that they see luxury products as a symbol of a high-quality and successful lifestyle, which not only engages them with luxury product ownership, but also the experience of the shopping process. In addition, the China Ones often mention that they have had great experiences in shopping for luxury goods abroad. They love to shop when they travel to other countries; the luxury products they bought became a part of their memory of the trip with friends and family.

• The China One interviewees also often bring up social connections gained through shopping, especially how they feel connected with their peers when they all bought the same brands or even the exact same products. "All of my girl friends have a Chanel Leboy Bag, I feel I will not fit in with them if I don't have one," said one girl during the interview. Another said: "Every time we have a party, everyone talks about what they bought since the last time we met. I love to bring the new bag or wear new shoes I have bought to the party. I feel I am the center of attention." As the only child in the family, the social life sometimes encourages China Ones to own more luxury products than they can afford. Because of the support of the "4-2-1" family, they are often given money by their parents and grandparents: "Sometimes, when I see somebody has something fancy and I cannot buy it by for myself, I will mention it to my family. When it comes to an occasion or a holiday celebration, they will give me money to buy it as a gift. I appreciate that they always want me to have the best and own the things my friends have." With the support of their family, China Ones are shopping without limits. An interviewee showed her Hermes "Birkin

Bag" to me and said: "This is not a bag, it is a ticket to the social club. If you don't have this kind of luxury goods (a high priced fine luxury product, usually refers to something above 50,000 RMB), you cannot make friends in the network." She also showed me a BV wallet and said: "I like this brand because I love the no-logo design, I use this and the people who know the brand and understand it will appreciate it. My friends all love it." The idea of wearing something only a few will understand – this is one of the findings from the interviews that shows one of the social motivations in China Ones' luxury shopping behaviors.

• A lot of the interviewees discussed that sometimes they purchase luxury products as gifts for their friends, family members or business partners. When they purchase luxury gifts, they tend to consider the attributes of the receivers' personality, occupations as well as social status. The gift shopping usually happens during Valentine's Day, Christmas, Chinese New Year or personal memorial dates of the receivers. Luxury gifts are popular because of high prices, outstanding design, quality and the reputation of the brands ensure the gifts' appreciation. During the interviews, the participants mentioned they are more likely buying leather goods, small accessories or perfume which do not require size/measurements information when purchasing as a gift.

2. BEST EXPERIENCE VS. THE DREAM LUXURY PRODUCT

This group includes the notes that relate to the best shopping experience and dream luxury products China Ones would like to purchase. As an informational interview section, the answers from this group show the feedback from China Ones' previous luxury goods shopping experiences as well as their expectations towards luxury purchasing in the future. The sub-group of "Best Experience" shows how China Ones choose their favorite luxury product and the shopping experience related with it. The sub-group of "The Dream Luxury Product" helps to understand the ultimate value and experience they are looking for as luxury customers. The outcome of this group will guide the further development of insights and strategy toward shopping experience and branding communication development that targets China Ones as a primary group of consumers.

During the research process, about 60 notes were categorized into this group, then further categorized into two sub-groups: "Best Experience" and "Dream Luxury Product." What follows are the detailed results for each sub-group analysis.

Sub-Group2-1: Best Luxury Shopping Experience

After further identification, about 40 notes were categorized in this sub-group. After grouping the related ones, the connections were drawn out on a white-board. The secondary research has discussed several case studies towards marketing strategies that luxury brands performed in China [see page 74]. This sub-group shows how China Ones responded regarding their luxury shopping experience. During the interview, the participants were asked to talk about their best experience with one brand, and why it was the best experience for them. Upon Hearing China Ones talking about their experience, and feeling the emotions they showed during interviews, four highlights of the responses were concluded and refined as follows:

• Most of the participants mentioned that their best luxury shopping experiences were the first luxury products they bought: Walking into a luxury brand store and being given a gift or shopping for themselves by using their first month's salary... Many memories are associated with these products, which make the products become iconic. The brands, which their first luxury products purchase represent, can become the favorite brands to which China Ones are loyal.

• Many China Ones mentioned during the interviews that they enjoy the experience of shopping for traditional luxury brands, which have a long history and heritage, as well as well-known designers who worked for these brands. An interviewee said, "I love LV, even if there are lot more new brands and other 'old' brands, I still love LV. The history behind the products and the consistent outstanding service they provide all the time makes LV my best experience each time I walk into their stores." Another interviewee said: "My best experience is the flagship store of Gucci in Shanghai. It is well designed and carries the best products. Gucci is a traditional brand. Some of my friends don't like it, but I do. I think the experience includes in-store and also on-line, the brand's appearance on both are always great."

• Many China One interviewees discussed that their best experiences of luxury shopping were shopping while traveling during vacation. "I love to shop in France, the "real" shopping place of luxury products. I will never forget the first time I walked in the Chanel store in Paris. It was a great experience to truly feel the brand's DNA as well as the brand heritage." Another China One said, "I love to shop while I am on business trips to other countries; the products I buy seems to last longer. I tend to use them more often, because I brought them all the way back home.

I want to see it in my closet and wear it. It makes me feel good, as if I am a successful traveling business man who is always on the run."

• Many participants mentioned they love to shop in boutiques instead of department stores, because the experience would always be better in the single brand operated stores. In addition, the interviewees also mentioned that they love to go to the newly opened designers' stores. An interviewee said, "Unlike the traditional brands, the contemporary brands have more cool feelings. They are very innovative and conceptual on their visual merchandising. I feel inspired and excited every time I go to these stores."

Sub-Group2-2: The Dream Luxury Product

The question "If you have the ability to buy any luxury product, what's your dream product?"was asked to all the participants. About 20 notes with answers were categorized in this sub-group, which shows China Ones' potential shopping focus and values toward the future. After analyzing the answers, there are three highlights listed as follows:

• The dream products were described differently between males and females. The male China Ones focused on automobiles, watches, formal apparel as well as experiential luxury product (travel) categories. The female China Ones focused on handbags, jewelry, and couture.

• Most of the participants had a specific product from a specific brand. "I want a white Porsche 911," one interviewee said during the interview. This finding shows the materialization of China Ones' luxury shopping values and the in-depth understanding of the brands they love.

• During the interviews, many participants mentioned "Customization." Their dream products were custom designed, one-of-a-kind products from their favorite brand. This shows the individualism of China One's value as well as the reason why products of limited editions are always popular within the China One group.

3. THESIS STUDY INSIGHTS VS. METHODS

While the interviewees were answering questions, some insights toward this thesis study and further analysis were generated on notes. This group includes the notes that relate to potential analysis methods as well as the ideas of how to further use the interview notes to develop strategies toward China Ones. The notes and the insights will be further used in the next steps. Some examples of "Insights – Method of Developing Strategy" are stated as follows:

• Necessity of Luxury Products – Maslow's Hierarchy of Needs Theory

An insight of the primary interview research shows that the level of necessity in luxury shopping is different with the secondary research results. China Ones "need" luxury products more than other luxury consumers in general. This insight will be further illustrated by refining Maslow's hierarchy of needs theory in the following strategy development section.

• Heritage Vs. Modern / On Trend – Adoption of Innovation

During the interviews, China Ones indicated that they have a unique point of view in defining luxury. They are searching for the balance between heritage and modern. They appreciate traditional culture and the history of luxury products as much as they are attracted by contemporary luxury brands. Diffusion of Innovation Theory[3] and its diagram is a great method to use to illustrate a group of consumer's reaction towards multiple product categories referred to as Diffusion of Fashion Innovation. In the following strategy building and analysis, this theory will be used to examine and show the comparison of adoption processes for luxury products and fashion products in the China One group.

• Emotional Connections in Motivation of Luxury Shopping – VALS based Segmentation / Profiling

During the research, the participants frequently showed their emotional connections between the luxury products and themselves, which shows the value of studying their motivation for consumption along with shopping behavior. VALS (short for "Values, Attitudes And Lifestyles")[4] is a customer behavior focused research methodology often used for psycho-graphic market segmentation. Base on the nine types of VALS consumer segmentation, a China One consumer behavior-based segmentation will be developed in the following analysis and strategy building section.

OBSERVATION

STORES' SELECTION

The objective of the observation is to examine and identify the current practice and promotion strategies of luxury brands in Chinese market in order to determine opportunities for them to better target and communicate with China Ones. Due to the limitation of time and resources, the observation was done within one month, taking place at 55 stores across six cities, which sell traditional luxury brands, up and coming luxury brands (contemporary designer brands) as well as affordable luxury brands. Figure 25 is an info-graphic including stores, locations and in-store pictures.

During the observation, the scale of the store, the interior, the visual merchandising as well as promotional materials were examined and compared within the same brand in different cities, as

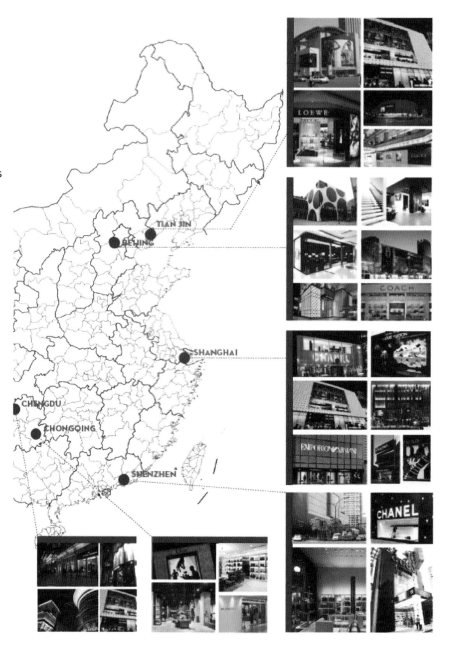

Figure 25 Observation Map

well as different brands in the same city. The highlights of the observations are listed as follows:

DIFFERENT LEVELS OF DEVELOPMENT IN BRAND INTEGRATION

During the observation in different cities, I found that there are more varieties of brands in Beijing and Shanghai than other cities. For example, there are stores such as Alexander Wang, Comme des Garcons, Celine and Miu Miu in Beijing; and Givenchy, Bottega Veneta in Shanghai, which are high fashion contemporary brands. In contrast, other visited cities mostly have traditional mainstream brands, such as Louis Vuitton, Gucci and Prada. This shows the different phases of luxury market development in different tier cities.

In addition, it is also confirmed during interviews with China Ones that the China Ones who live in the developed cities have different luxury good shopping perspectives than China Ones who live in other cities. Even though on-line shopping has been well adopted by China Ones, physical stores' appearance is still important because the accessibility of brands is directly related with the awareness of the brands' impact and sales of the brands in the area.

GROWING FOCUS ON AFFORDABLE BRANDS

Through in-store observations, it was found that many affordable brands have developed awareness of the consumers and have gained sales in the past three years. From the First Tier cites to Third Tier cities, affordable brands such as Coach and Michael Kors have successfully attracted more in-store traffic to compete with traditional brands. Moreover, according to observations of in-store activities, there are more customers buying products from affordable brands than traditional luxury brands. This phenomenon shows how the competitive price points of the affordable brands' impact their growth of market shares in the Chinese Market.

In order to confirm the China Ones' opinions toward affordable brands, they were asked to share their thoughts on these brands. Demonstrating a positive attitude towards affordable brands, China Ones agree that affordable luxury brands bridge the gap between fashion products and luxury products. Most of them bought affordable brand products for their daily usage as well as gifts for friends and family members because of both the affordable price points as well as well-established brand image and awareness.

THE DISTRIBUTION AND OPERATION OF LUXURY BRAND STORES

CHINA ONE, THE LOVE OF THE LUXE

During the observation in six cities, it is found that most of the luxury brands have chosen the shopping centers or downtown tourism areas to open their stores. The luxury brands are concentrated in one or more high profile shopping malls. Most of the brands have in-store boutiques operated by similar Chinese luxury brand distributors. This operational model ensures a consistency of brand image as well as uniform service across the brands in different cities.

During the interviews, China Ones showed positive feedback on the operations of luxury brands in China. They expect the same brand to have the same representations in different cities, which is very important to the in-store shopping experience. They also pointed out that they prefer the luxury stores located in the fashion district together with other brands and stores rather than isolated outside of this shopping zone.

THE SHOPPING ENVIRONMENT AND EXPERIENCE OF IN-STORE LUXURY SHOPPING

During the observation within 55 luxury stores of different brands and different scales, it is found that most of the luxury brands have tailored their merchandise for the Chinese luxury customers. For example, most of the brands maintain a high volume of their well-known products/items, which are classic and basic styles. Also, the colors of the products are carefully chosen in order to gain more sales during China's holiday seasons: for instance, the color red is considered a sign of wealth, happiness and luck for the Chinese. The observations took place before the Christmas and New Year holidays. Most of the stores had many red and pink products in their major display areas to drive sales of holiday gifting.

During the secret shopping in stores, it was found that most of the sales assistants provided outstanding services to the customers. However, some of the traditional luxury brands' sale associates showed different attitudes by judging customers' outfits to determine their income and probability of buying products. China Ones confirmed this finding during interviews. They pointed out that they would always dress up to go to luxury stores for browsing or shopping, because they will get better service from the sale associates.

BRAND IN-STORE INTERIOR DESIGNS AND PROMOTIONAL MATERIALS

During this observation, many brands showed well-designed store interiors and floor layouts, which delivered a luxurious message to their customers. In most of the flagship stores, there are VIP fitting rooms and lounges.

Most of the RTW or couture brand stores have in-house tailors who provide re-sizing services. Many stores offer free gift-wrapping services during the holiday season to provide exceptional services to their customers.

There are many in-store promotional materials collected during observations. Most of the materials are from traditional luxury brands who have larger budgets for print material promotions; many designer brands and affordable brands do not have printed look-books or brochures; instead, their sale associates would refer to the website for information.

CONCLUSION OF PRIMARY RESEARCH

In summation, the primary research is designed, practiced, and analyzed in order to fill the gap in the lack of direct evidence and information for China Ones' luxury shopping behaviors.

On-line surveys provided solid data of basic information of China Ones' income and luxury-shopping preferences. In-person interviews provide the reasons behind the data by deeply examining China Ones' motivations and values toward luxury shopping. In-store observations collected the information and visual evidence of how the current luxury bands in China are operating and promoting themselves as well as China Ones' feedback toward branding and shopping experiences. The findings and insights developed from the primary research will be combined with the results of secondary research to further guide the framework and strategy development for luxury brands to implement in order to better communicate with China Ones.

NOTES

1. In China, the Tier One cities are the most important cities based on the size of their middle income to affluent population (defined as those with a monthly household income of RMB 5,000 and above). On average, each of these cities is home to around 3 million adults from households with a monthly income of RMB 5,000 and above. The Tier Two cities are a bit lower then the Tier One, which is between 3,500 to 5,000 RMB. Each of these cities has a relevant urban population (middle or upper income adults) of over 350,000 people.

2. "Luxury Experiences in China - A KPMG Study | KPMG | CN," May 6, 2011, accessed May 17, 2013, http://www.kpmg.com/cn/en/issuesandinsights/articlespublications/pages/luxury-experiences-in-china-201105.aspx.

3. Diffusion of innovations is a theory that seeks to explain how, why, and at what rate new ideas and technology spread through cultures. Everett Rogers, a professor of communication studies, popularized the theory in his book *Diffusion of Innovations*; the book was first published in 1962, and is now in its fifth edition (2003). Rogers, E. M. (2003). Diffusion of innovations (5th edition). New York, NY: Free Press.

4. VALS ("Values, Attitudes And Lifestyles") is a proprietary research methodology used for psycho-graphic market segmentation. Market segmentation is designed to guide companies in tailoring their products and services in order to appeal to the people most likely to purchase them.VALS was developed in 1978 by social scientist and consumer futurist Arnold Mitchell and his colleagues at SRI.

Chapter 6

TAKE A NEW LOOK AT CHINA ONE
– Frameworks and Strategies Development toward China One Luxury Consumption

In examining the development of marketing analysis frameworks and strategies, there are many classic methodologies that are used through different periods of time toward different markets. However, the situation varies in different markets and products: Based on primary and secondary research, the China One groups need luxury brands to tailor specific frameworks to effectively develop and implement marketing strategies. This chapter will present marketing models that will support those strategies for the China One segment.

MAPPING CHINA ONES' LUXURY SHOPPING VALUE SYSTEM THROUGH EXISTING MODELS
MASLOW'S REFINED HIERARCHY OF NEEDS OF CHINA ONES

THE FRAMEWORKS AND THE RELATIONSHIP WITH THE CHINA ONE GROUP

Figure 26 Diagram of Maslow's Hierarchy of Needs

As figure 26 shows, the theory of Maslow's Hierarchy of Needs[1] is a psychological study created by Abraham Maslow and first discussed in his paper "A Theory of Human Motivation" in 1943. Maslow describes the needs from basic to advanced by using the terms physiological, safety, belongingness and love, esteem, and self-actualization.

During the primary and secondary research, it was found that China Ones grew up with superior material conditions that awakened the needs of basic biological and physiological needs. Raised by four grandparents and two parents, China Ones always have strong support for shelter and protection, which weakens their safety

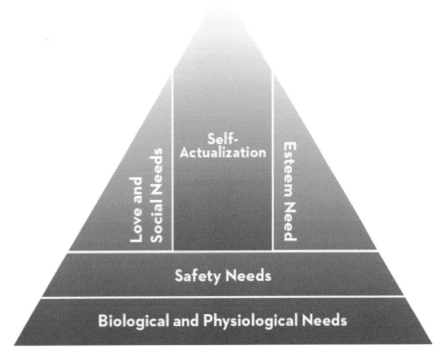

Figure 27 Refined Hierarchy of Needs Model towards China One

needs. On the other hand, as the only child in the family, China Ones grew up without siblings, which makes China Ones have a strong need for love and social connections, reputation and status, as much as the need from self actualization. As figure 27 illustrates, according to the uniqueness of China Ones' background and physiological need findings, the Hierarchy of Needs are refined with fewer Needs in the first two basic needs but more Needs in the top three levels. In addition, instead of having three levels listed as low to high, the China Ones' Hierarchy of Needs diagram has three horizontally distributed Needs on the top of the triangle in order to emphasize the importance of Love and Social as well as Esteem Needs.

IMPLEMENTATION INTO LUXURY MARKETING STRATEGY

One of the most important attributes of products in general is to fulfill the needs of the consumer. As figure 28 shows, the difference between Maslow's original theory and the refined China One's needs' model is the social focus of China Ones' high level needs.

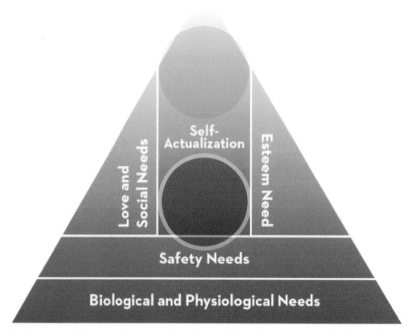

Figure 28 China One's Luxury Consumption Needs Move Down to the Middle of the Triangle

Luxury products, in normal scenarios, will be fulfilling the Self-Actualization needs (on the top of the model) because of the attributes of luxury goods – unnecessary, high price, relations with ownership, rewarding and self-image display. However, for China Ones, according to the research results [see Chapter Five] and findings, luxury products become necessary because of their specific needs of belonging, social networking as well as self-actualization. In the refined model [figure 27], the needs for purchasing luxury products will move down to the middle of the triangle.

From unnecessary to necessary, this change of China Ones' need for luxury products is a key for the development of a marketing strategy. Instead of marketing or promoting the needs and wants of luxury goods, the luxury brands should focus on how to promote luxury products as an expression of self-image, a way of self-rewarding as well as a social experience that should be shared with peers and friends. By changing the focus of the marketing and promotion strategy, luxury brands would potentially fulfill China Ones' higher level of social and self-actualization in order to perhaps drive sales increases.

THE DIFFUSION OF INNOVATION

THE MODEL AND THE RELATIONSHIP WITH THE CHINA ONE GROUP

Diffusion of innovations[2] is a theory discussed by Everett Rogers in his book *Diffusion of Innovations*[3] in 2003. As figure 29 below shows, the theory is often used to explain the process, the reason and the rate a new idea or a new product is diffused through society. In most of the situations, the theory is often used for technology related products and ideas.

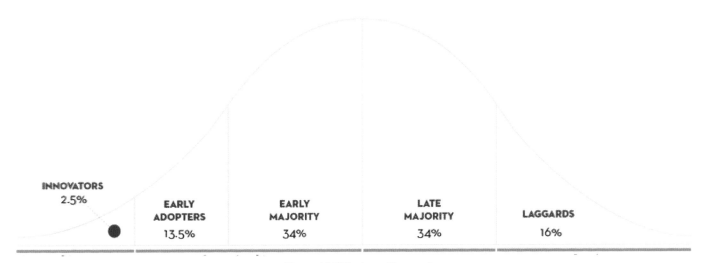

Figure 29 Diffusion of innovations

There are many ways of implementing the theory and putting it into practice. In this paper, this theory is used to show the level of innovation of the China One group as a consumer. Also, later in the paper, this model will also be used to illustrate the lifestyle of different fashion related products compared with China One's adoption cycle.

The theory of Diffusion of Innovation maintains four main elements that influence the process of an innovation's diffusion: The innovation (idea or product), the communication channels, time period, and a social system. Using this theory on China Ones' luxury consumption, the four elements will be:

• The innovation: New luxury products

• The communication Channels: In-store and On-line

• Time Period: Luxury product life cycle in general

• Social System: Mainland China

According to the secondary research and primary research, the China Ones adopt new trends and luxury products faster than consumers in China on average. They live with a fast paced Internet-oriented lifestyle that allows access to a variety of new products and new trends everyday. They are open to new brands and new products. Within the theory diagram, the China One group will mostly fill the first three groups of adapters: The innovator, the early adopters and early majority. According to previous secondary research, the China One group is the mainstream consumer group in China. This group characteristic of China Ones could be a key when luxury brands are developing a luxury market strategy toward the Chinese market.

IMPLEMENTATION INTO LUXURY MARKETING STRATEGY

According to the secondary and primary research, the luxury products can be further divided by the different lengths of a products' cycle: Classic, On-trend and Fad:

1). The Classic: The Classic Luxury Product Category includes the products that maintain a basic style and design which are sold every season. This category of luxury products is usually the introductory products for the first-time luxury consumers.

2). The On-trend: The On-trend Luxury Product Category includes the products of each season. This category's products are designed to represent current trends and new technology, which is also the main category of luxury products.

3). The Fad: The Fad Luxury Product Category includes the products of limited editions, special collections as well as collectable pieces sold only in a short amount of time. The cycle of this category of luxury products are the shortest, compared with Classic and On-trend products.

According to the primary and secondary research insights and findings, figure 30 below shows the sales distributed in each adopter's group. The first three groups of China Ones' domain show that because of the level of adoption and ability of luxury consumption, China Ones are the main purchasing consumer of Fad and On-trend product categories. In contrast, China Ones are not the group buying the most basic, classic styled luxury products in the Chinese market. This insight provides a guide for developing a marketing strategy towards China Ones. The brands need to focus on promoting the limited editions and current seasonal trendy products and special collections to China Ones in order to increase the sales towards both Fad and On-trend Categories.

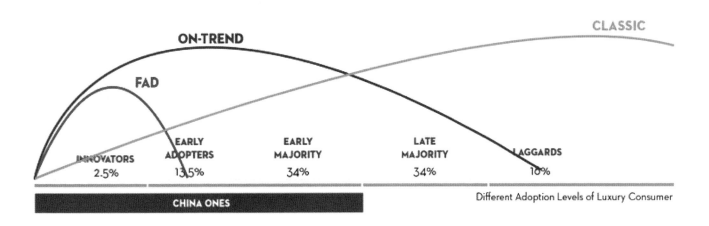

Figure 30 A Generalization of China Ones' Luxury Products Adoption Curve

CHINA ONE LUXURY CONSUMER PROFILING
CHINA ONE LUXURY CONSUMER SEGMENTATION

THE VALS MODEL AND THE RELATIONSHIP WITH CHINA ONE GROUP

VALS[3] divides consumers into eight lifestyle segments. The VALS framework is focused on primary motivation and resources based on segmentation development. According to the primary and secondary research, the China Ones are more innovative than average Chinese luxury consumers; also, with the support of their "4-2-1 Family,"

China Ones tend to have more spending power to purchase luxury products than other generations.

As figure 31 shows, the China One luxury consumer could be categorized into the top four groups that have higher innovation attention and resources. Based on this categorization and primary research insights related to motivation, China One Luxury Consumer Segmentation is developed in the section covered in red.

CHINA ONE LUXURY CONSUMER SEGMENTATION

Market segmentations are designed to guide companies

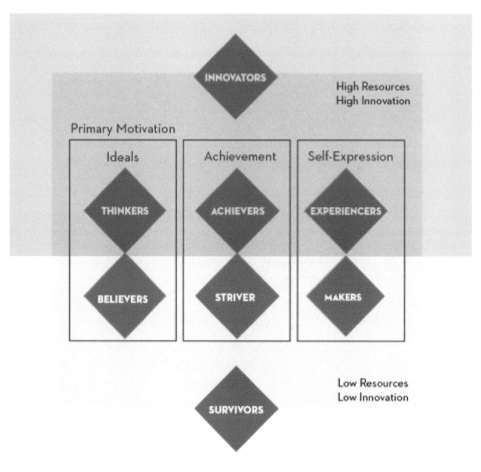

Figure 31 China Ones' Segmentation in VALS System

in tailoring their products and services in order to fulfill the needs of the consumer. As figure 32 shows below, this segmentation of China One Luxury Consumers is created based on both VALS motivation segmentation and primary research results of China Ones' main attributes of luxury consumption motivation. This LSEDP segmentation has five segments, which are L-Expert, Self-Glories, Experimenter, Diplomatist and Pragmatist (from most involved with luxury lifestyle to less involved), so called LSEDP for short. The details of segmentation are listed as follow:

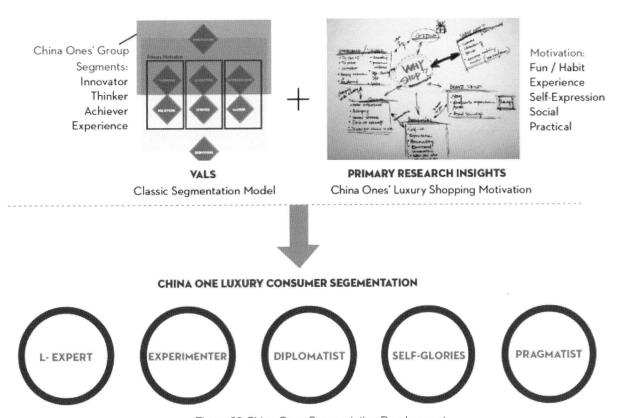

Figure 32 China Ones Segmentation Development

L-Expert (L-专家)

L-Expert is close to the innovator in the VALS system; the most highly evolved luxury consumers, they have rich knowledge of many luxury brands and up-coming trends. Buying luxury products for collecting and ownership as a habit are key perspectives of L-Experts toward luxury products. They usually have a fashion related or creative oriented job and have good taste and a good eye as well. They are not loyal to one or several brands; instead, they tend to buy products they like from a variety of brands across different price points. For the L-Expert, the style and material are more important than the brand.

In demographic terms, according to the primary research's 218 samples, most of the people in this segment are women. More than half of the people in this segment are living in First Tier cities. They have higher income than average and have more luxury purchasing power than other segments.

Self-Glories (自赏家)

Self-Glories is the segment most highly affluent and dedicated to maintaining a luxury lifestyle. The luxury products they buy are mostly to match their image, status and taste. They love to buy "no-logo-displayed" luxury products because they are buying the products for themselves as rewards and tools for reducing pressure from jobs. The Self-Glories always buy luxury products that remind them of themselves and that they have an emotional connection with. The brand's image and heritage is very important to them when they are making purchasing decisions. They are loyal customers of certain brands. After their first successful purchase from one brand, and if the products and services satisfiy the Self-Glories, they would more likely go back to purchase its products again.

According to primary research results, in this segment, there are more women than men. The segment has an average age (about 29 years old) that is older than other segments with higher income.

Experimenter (实验家)

Powered by the motive of searching for meaningful memories and new experiences, the Experimenters have the least materialistic orientation among the segments. The products' brands, history, and even the products themselves are not that important for Experimenters, but it is the process of purchasing that appeals to them.

How did they buy it; who they bought it with; when they bought it, it is the story behind the purchase. When Experimenters are asked questions like those, they will not stop talking. The fun, the memories and the mood of the purchasing day are what maintained each luxury product. In addition, Experimenters are the most technology heavy segments: They will be those people waiting on-line to buy new luxury electronic products. To be the first one to try new things is the key motive of their purchase of luxury products. Moreover, Experimenters love to purchase experiential luxury products, such as luxury vacations, tours, and spa treatments. For them, the experience is more important then any other matter.

The majority of the Experimenters are men. The age and geographic distribution is even to all ages of China Ones in many cities that cross First Tier, Second Tier and other cities as well.

Diplomatist (外交家)

Diplomatist is the segment with the most social-oriented motivations toward luxury shopping. They are highly attuned to On-trend brands and believe luxury is best expressed in what they buy and what they own. Luxury shopping for them is more like a social activity. Shopping with friends, trying things on and talking about the feedback is the key of Diplomatist segments' focus of their luxury shopping activities. Their luxury choices follow the trends created by the media, brands and public, rather than being based on their own feelings and understanding of luxury products and specific brands. They somehow are buying luxury products and wearing them for others to see and to appreciate. The social motivation of luxury purchasing is the key significance of this segment.

The age range of this segment, most of whom are women, is mostly distributed in the range of 22-27 years old. The Second Tier and other cities have more Diplomatists than First Tier cities. The income varies widely and the amount of money spent on luxury shopping varies as well.

Pragmatist (实用家)

The Pragmatist is a newly emerged type of luxury consumer who is not entirely involved in the luxury lifestyle. Although they can afford luxury products, they don't care about luxury brands and trends that are promoted through advertising. They are focusing on the functionality and the usability of the product. They are buying luxury products with a clear criteria. The buying decision is based on their needs and if the product fulfills these needs. Sometimes, they are buying luxury products as gifts for friends or business partners, which makes them become seasonal consumers who are more active in the holiday season. They are price-rational consumers who will always do research before they go to stores or on-line stores to buy the products.

In gender terms, this is the most male dominated segment out of all five (68 percent). According to the primary research, most of the people in this segment are men. In addition, this is the group that has the most percentage of luxury purchasing on gifting, which usually happens in the holiday seasons.

SUMMARY: CHINA ONE LUXURY CONSUMER SEGMENTATION – "LSEDP"

In examining the differences among LSEDP segmentation, there are many ways to illustrate it with the existing model in order to better explain the differences and similarities between each segment. Several perspectives of illustrations are shown as follows:

LSEDP IN MOTIVATION/INVOLVEMENT MATRIX MAP AND STRATEGY DEVELOPMENT ACCORDING TO THE POSITIONING:

The four significant correlations that played major roles in identifying each segment are: High/Low Involvement of Luxury Lifestyle and High/Low Motivations toward Social/ Status. In order to further develop effective marketing strategies to target each segment, understanding the motivation and the level of social involvement toward luxury consumption are the key.

As figure 33 shows, the L-Expert is the most involved of luxury lifestyle groups. The marketing strategy towards L-Experts should focus on promoting luxury lifestyle as well as balance between self-expression and socialization by emphasizing the value of the brands and products.

The Self-Glories segment has the lowest motivation toward socialization; instead, this segment mostly focuses on self-image matching as well as self-expression in a high quality lifestyle. The marketing strategy towards Self-Glories should focus on promoting the products' attributes of high quality and value-adding benefits.

The Experimenter segment has a balance between each correlation. The people in this segment are heavy users

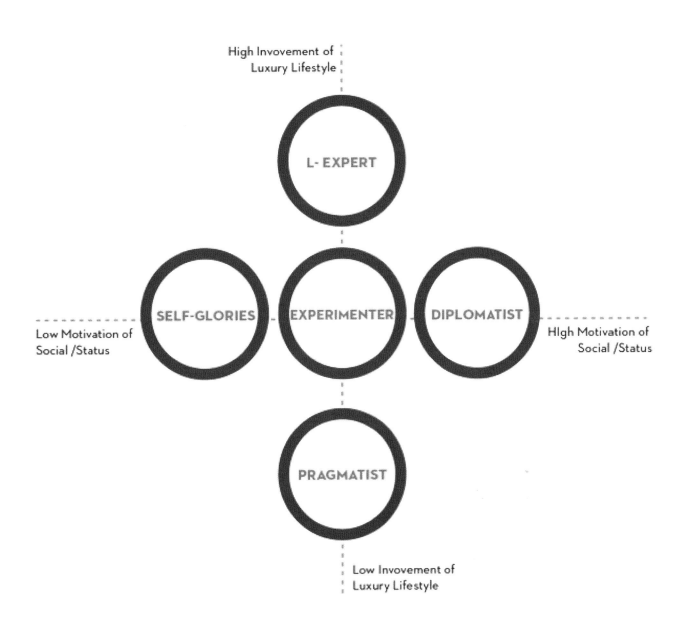

Figure 33 LSEDP in Motivation/Involvement Matrix

of technology and other innovative products. They tend to purchase more experiential products than other segments. When targeting this segment, the marketing strategy needs to focus on multiple channel promotion, especially social media promotions. The content needs to emphasize "What's new" in order to encourage the Experimenters to buy.

The Diplomatist segment has the highest motivation toward socialization. This significance shows that the marketing strategy built around this group needs to concentrate on using influential media, news, and celebrities to create the social buzz of the products in order to attract Diplomatist's attention to create the "wants" of luxury purchasing.

The Pragmatist is the segment that has the least involvement in a luxury lifestyle. It is the only group who buys luxury products because of needs. Marketing strategy building towards this segment needs to emphasize the product's functionality, quality, materials, convenient design and positive reviews from previous customers in order to encourage the Pragmatist to purchase.

LSEDP IN REFINED HIERARCHY OF NEEDS DIAGRAM

According to the uniqueness of China Ones' background and physiological needs findings, the Hierarchy of Needs was refined in the previous analysis. In order to demonstrate the relationship between LSEDP and the root of the need and incentive, figure 34 shows how the segmentation interacts with the new Hierarchy of Needs diagram. In the diagram, the L-Expert and Self-Glories are in the top part of Self-Actualization because of the high concentration of self-value and rewarding. The segment of Experimenter and Pragmatist are on the lower level of the Self-Actualization section because of the lower involvement in a luxury lifestyle. The Diplomatist is on both sides of Love & Social Needs and Esteem Needs because of the high involvement of social motivations of their luxury shopping behavior. This combined diagram will further guide the development of a marketing strategy from marketing mix (4Ps) perspective.

LSEDP IN LUXURY PRODUCTS ADOPTION CURVE

As the previous section discussed, the China Ones are a dominant luxury consumer group which fits into the first three phases of luxury products adoption curve. Figure 35 shows how the LSEDP segmentation performs on the

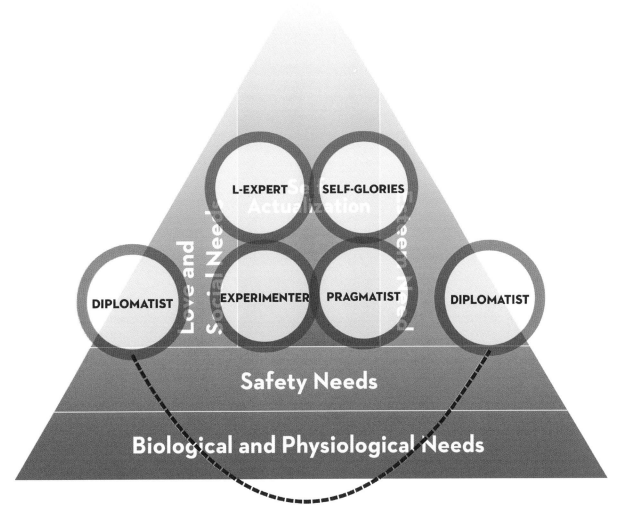

Figure 34 LSEDP in New Maslow's Theory Diagram

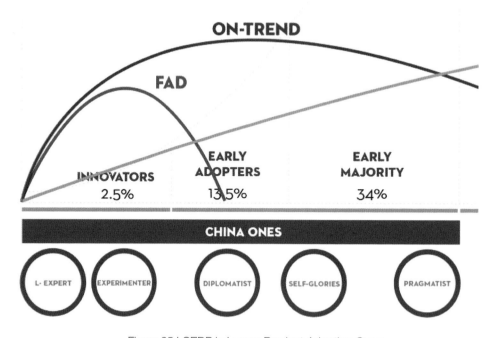

Figure 35 LSEDP in Luxury Product Adoption Curve

adoption of luxury products' life-cycle curve.

As the figure 35 shows, the L-Expert and Experimenter segments are listed as innovators due to the high level involvement in lifestyle by the L-Expert as well as the innovative adopting ability of the Experimenter. These two groups are the main consumers of limited edition products as well as the new technology oriented luxury products.

The Diplomatist and Self-Glories are the dominant groups of Early Adopters. They are making purchasing decisions after the reviews of the products are out on the market. They are more likely to buy luxury products that have good customer feedback after celebrities or trend leaders use them. The difference between these two segments is that the Diplomatists are buying to catch up with the trend; the Self-Glories are buying after they do research and making sure the product is the right fit for their styles.

The Pragmatists are mostly in the third group – Early Majority – because they don't care about luxury brands and trends that are promoted through advertising for each season. Not only do they focus on the functionality and the usability of the product, but they are buying luxury products with clear criteria – the usability and functions – so that they always tend to buy the luxury products after many people have tried them and provided positive feedback.

PERSONA STUDY OF EACH SEGMENTATION

After examining the significance of the LSEDP segmentation, in order to provide a vivid representation of different China One's type within a specific demographic, geographic as well as lifestyle visualization. By using lifestyle boarding, each segment's persona study is listed as follows:

Figure 36 LSEDP Persona Study Overview

L-expert "L-专家"

LSEDP Segmentation Persona Study

"I appreciate Luxury goods as I appreciate life. I collect them and make them as a part of myself. Can't live without them, not only because I love them, but also because I tell my story through them."

-Ceci Cheng

DEMOGRAPHIC

Age	City	Education	Occupation	Annual Income	Marital Status
3x	Shanghai	MBA	PR Manager	320,000RMB	In relationship

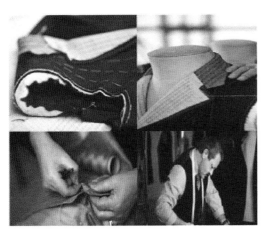

PSYCHOGRAPHIC

Social Media

Weibo(Chinese Twitter),
Instagram
WeChat

Spare-time

Travel
Gallery Events
Yoga

Can't live without

Camera when traveling
Hermes Planner
VCA watch

LUXURY SHOPPING HABITS

Information Channel

Magazine
Fashion Blog
Instagram

Shopping Channel

Luxury Shopping Mall
Net-a-Porter
Luxury Boutique

Monthly Expenses

Avg
15,000RMB on Luxury Goods

Figure 37 LSEDP Persona Study 1

Self-Glories "自赏家"

LSEDP Segmentation Persona Study

"I buy those luxury goods that I can 'feel' it. I love the no-logo-displayed products because I don't want to show off. I wear it and only the person who has the same taste with me will understand its value and the spirits behind it."

-Rachel Huang

DEMOGRAPHIC

Age	City	Education	Occupation	Annual Income	Marital Status
29	Beijing	BBA of Marketing	Dr. of Marketing	240,000RMB	Single

PSYCHOGRAPHIC

Social Media

Weibo(Chinese Twitter),
Instagram
Douban, Wechat

Spare-time

Cooking
Reading
Swimming

Can't live without

Simi (Cat)
Vintage Coat
Tiffany Ring

LUXURY SHOPPING HABITS

Information Channel

On-line Fashion Websites
Magazine
Weibo

Shopping Channel

Oversea Agency
On-line Stores
DFS

Monthly Expenses

Avg
10,000RMB on Luxury Goods

Figure 38 LSEDP Persona Study 2

Experimenter "实验家"

LSEDP Segmentation Persona Study

"I believe the excitement of life is to try new things. I always want to be the first one get to use new products or services. I love unique stuff, it makes me feel I am special. I am a collector, the products I brought help me remember the moments of my life."

-Jeff Zhao

DEMOGRAPHIC

Age	City	Education	Occupation	Annual Income	Marital Status
27	Shanghai	BS of Computer	UX Designer	130,000RMB	Single

PSYCHOGRAPHIC

Social Media

Weibo
WeChat
Solidot

Spare-time

Biking
Photography
Web Development

Can't live without

Laptop
BlackMagic Camera
Bike

LUXURY SHOPPING HABITS

Information Channel

Fashion & Tech Blog
Oversea Trend Report
Lifestyle Magazine

Shopping Channel

Shopping Mall
Online Lifestyle Stores
Lifestyle Boutiques

Monthly Expenses

Avg
6500RMB on Luxury Goods

Figure 39 LSEDP Persona Study 3

Diplomatist "外交家"

LSEDP Segmentation Persona Study

"I love to buy luxury products and wear/carry them everyday. It tells who I am and shows my taste to friends. I love to go shopping with friends. For me, luxury shopping is not only to buy it, but also something fun to do with friends."
-Sophia Chen

DEMOGRAPHIC

Age	City	Education	Occupation	Annual Income	Marital Status
25	Chengdu	BA of Hospitality Mgmt	Secretary	90,000RMB	In relationship

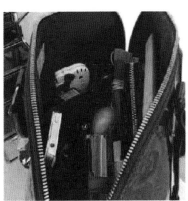

PSYCHOGRAPHIC

Social Media

Weibo(Chinese Twitter),
WeChat
RenRen

Spare-time

Clubbing
Shopping
Make-up Artist

Can't live without

Chanel Purse
Casio Camera
Walk-in Closet

LUXURY SHOPPING HABITS

Information Channel

Wechat
Fashion Magazine
Fashion Blog

Shopping Channel

Luxury Shopping Mall
Oversea Agency
Second-hand Luxury Boutique

Monthly Expenses

Avg
6,000RMB on Luxury Goods

Figure 40 LSEDP Persona Study 4

Pragmatist "实用家"

LSEDP Segmentation Persona Study

"I love to buy luxury products because I believe in the fine materials and the craftsmanship carried by the products. I usually buy luxury goods if I really need it or to give to my friends, my girlfriend and family members as a nice gift through the holiday seasons."

- Kane Liu

DEMOGRAPHIC

Age	City	Education	Occupation	Annual Income	Marital Status
30	Shenzhen	MS of Engineering	IT Manager	150,000RMB	Engaged

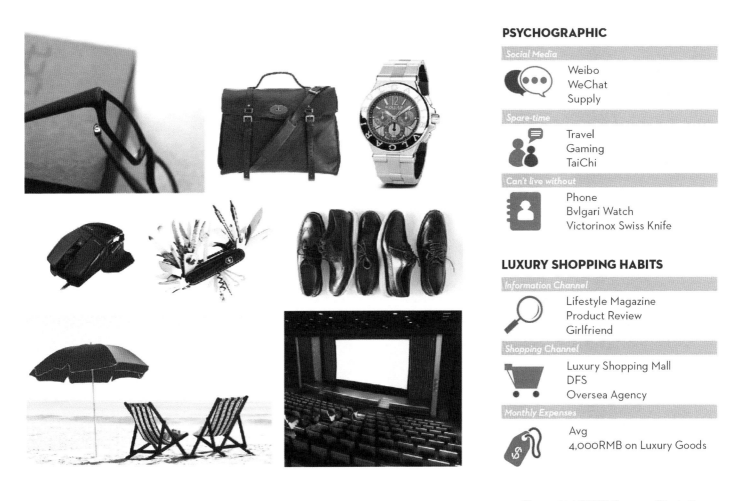

PSYCHOGRAPHIC

Social Media

Weibo
WeChat
Supply

Spare-time

Travel
Gaming
TaiChi

Can't live without

Phone
Bvlgari Watch
Victorinox Swiss Knife

LUXURY SHOPPING HABITS

Information Channel

Lifestyle Magazine
Product Review
Girlfriend

Shopping Channel

Luxury Shopping Mall
DFS
Oversea Agency

Monthly Expenses

Avg
4,000RMB on Luxury Goods

Figure 41 LSEDP Persona Study 5

RECOMMENDATIONS OF MARKETING STRATEGY TOWARD THE CHINA ONES
STRATEGY BUILDING BASED ON MARKETING MIX AND CHINA ONE'S NEEDS

In order to further implement the research results as well as the frameworks based on them, a refined marketing mix diagram was created according to China One's New Maslow Needs Theory.

As figure 42 shows, according to the different levels of Needs from the China One's refined Maslow Needs Diagram, each of the marketing mix elements is placed with the similar level of the needs matching the level of marketing elements from basic to advanced. For example:

The product is the core element of the marketing mix and is placed in the center of the triangle. It represents a tight connection with the value behind it as well as the brand image of the product.

Price and Place are two basic elements of the marketing mix, which are placed on the lower part of the triangle. The Price as an element sets up the accessibility of the product. The Place sets up the flexibility of the distribution channels of luxury products.

Promotion is placed on the top part of the triangle which shows the higher level of fulfillment of the Needs to its consumer. Promotion is the element related with the Needs of self-actualization, love and esteem. As luxury products, the consumer are normally not buying for needs, but buying for want. The promotion strategy in the marketing mix will create the desirability of the products.

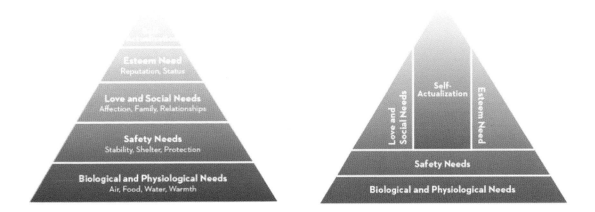

Figure 42 Marketing Mix Attributes Based on China One's Needs

As figure 43 shows, the following sections will list the recommendations for building a marketing strategy based on the combined diagram.

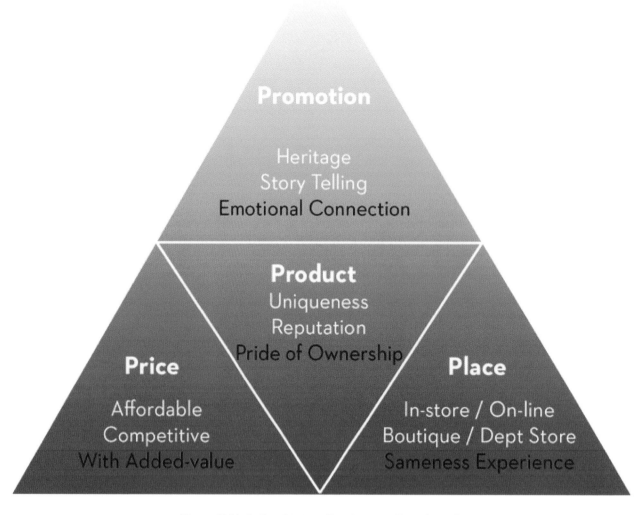

Figure 43 Marketing Strategy Development Based on 4Ps

MARKETING MIX ELEMENT STRATEGIES TARGETING THE CHINA ONES

MARKETING STRATEGY TOWARD PRODUCT

Among the marketing mix, the product is the most fundamental element, which is an item or a service that satisfies consumers' demands. For a product centric luxury marketing strategy, it is critical to understand the nature of the product, the value behind it, as well as the brand image that is related to it.

When targeting China Ones, the product's strategy should concentrate on developing unique products that stand out from the competition. Moreover, the reputation of the brand is also important for marketers to build in order to develop loyalty with their customers. In sum, the strategy should encourage the feeling of pride in ownership as a sign of a successful, high quality lifestyle.

MARKETING STRATEGY TOWARD PRICE

Price is an element of the marketing mix to create the possibility of purchasing. With luxury goods, marketers need to always carefully consider the price point. An over-priced luxury product compared with a competitor will cause low purchasing motivation. Also, an under-priced luxury product will lose the privilege and luxurious attributes of other luxury products.

When targeting in on China Ones, the pricing strategy needs to be built based on the cost of the product, the competitor's price as well as the reputation of the brands. The new emerging luxury brands usually start with a lower price point which helps the brands build marketing shares as well as the awareness of the brand. Some of the affordable luxury brands are gaining more consumers because of the affordable price point. Differentiated from these brands, the traditional brands should focus on adding value to services as well as consumer-relationship-developing events to further build a long-term value adding marketing strategy.

MARKETING STRATEGY TOWARD PLACE

With the growth of e-commerce and on-line shopping, the consumer now can shop for anything they want 24/7. This creates the extension of shopping hours and the easy access of luxury products from anywhere all over the world. As a luxury product marketer, it is important for brands to understand the consumer's shopping channels.

When targeting in on China Ones, the marketing strategy towards promotion needs to primarily understand the information channels, distribution channels, and payment methods. Where China Ones get information, where they shop and how they pay for the products are not always cohesively the same. So the marketing strategy toward Place needs to be considered separately than as a whole, because the overall brand's experience needs to be the same in order to deliver the same message, communicating in a timely manner with the consumer.

MARKETING STRATEGY TOWARD PROMOTION

At the top of the triangle, Promotion is located to indicate a higher level of interaction and communication with the consumer. The purpose of Promotion is aimed to create a dialogue with the existing and potential customers, based on their needs and lifestyles.

When targeting in on the China Ones, the marketing strategy towards Promotion needs to understand the deep motivation of the consumer's purchasing behaviors. From the brand, to culture, then to the story behind it, marketers need to create a story-telling strategy that helps bridge the communication with China Ones, further helping them to build the emotional connections with the brand and its product.

FROM THE 4PS TO THE 7PS

In addition to the 4Ps marketing mix towards China One's Luxury consumption, as figure 44 shows, there are three elements added in the diagram: people, policy, and perception.

The People: In order to succeed in the China-One-group-focused marketing activities, it is important to understand the stakeholders involved and their shopping behavior. The LSEDP segmentation is developed based on China Ones' shopping motivations. It is a great tool to unitize during marketing and promotion strategy development.

The Policy: As secondary research results show [see Chapters Two and Three], the significances of Chinese luxury market require the marketers to understand the unique political environment and related principles that guide their market strategies. It is an indispensable element to consider in order to ensure the feasibility of the strategy in China's market.

The Perception: Nothing in the world is immutable, as is marketing strategy. As one of the most important

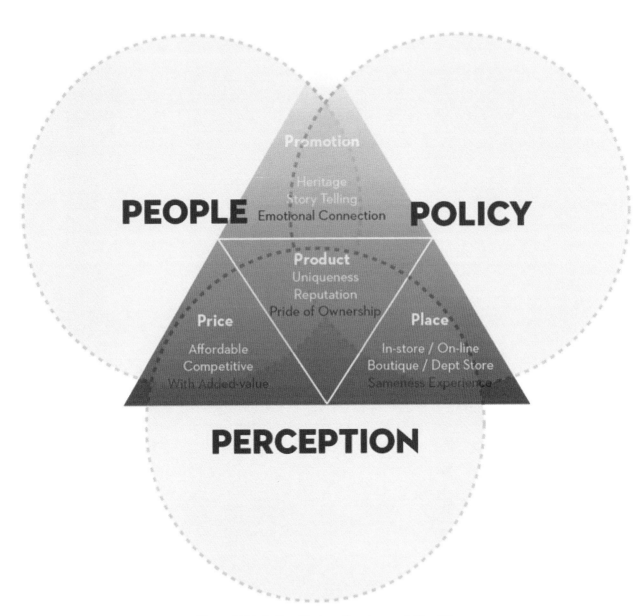

PEOPLE   **POLICY**

Promotion

Heritage
Story Telling
Emotional Connection

Product
Uniqueness
Reputation
Pride of Ownership

Price

Affordable
Competitive
With Added-value

Place

In-store / On-line
Boutique / Dept Store
Sameness Experience

PERCEPTION

Figure 44 Marketing Strategy Development- The 7Ps

elements in the 7Ps, perception emphasizes the dynamic of strategy that changes to fit the needs of the ever-changing market. There are many attributes that influence the changes of China One's behavior in the Chinese luxury market. To identify the changes and predict the next up-and-coming trend is crucial to the success of marketing luxury products toward the China One group.

NOTES

1. The Third Force: The Psychology of Abraham Maslow, By Frank G. Goble.

2. Diffusion of innovations is a theory that seeks to explain how, why, and at what rate new ideas and technology spread through cultures. Everett Rogers, a professor of communication studies, popularized the theory in his book Diffusion of Innovations; the book was first published in 1962, and is now in its fifth edition (2003). Rogers, E. M. (2003). Diffusion of innovations (5th edition). New York, NY: Free Press.

3. VALS ("Values, Attitudes And Lifestyles") is a proprietary research methodology used for psycho-graphic market segmentation. Market segmentation is designed to guide companies in tailoring their products and services in order to appeal to the people most likely to purchase them.The VALS method was developed by Arnold Mitchell and his colleagues in 1978. "VALS", Strategic Business Insights, http://www.strategicbusinessinsights.com/vals/, Assessed 2014.

Chapter 7

WHAT'S NEXT?
– Recommendations and Future Directions

The image of China Ones as individuals as well as a group of luxury consumers is coming together. However, the China One group is a dynamic generation with an innovative mindset. In order to better target the China Ones, it is not only necessary but also very important to understand the future direction of this group as consumers. This chapter will discuss the Critical Path for the future direction as the conclusion of this thesis.

FUTURE INFLUENCES OF CHINESE GOVERNMENT POLICIES TO CHINA ONES' LUXURY SHOPPING BEHAVIOR
THE LOOSENING OF THE ONE CHILD POLICY

At the end of 2013, the Chinese government announced the loosening of its One-Child Policy after more than 30 years of its establishment. As the *New York Times* discusses in its Asian News Section, "For decades, most urban couples have been restricted to having one child. That has been changing fitfully, with rules on the books that couples can have two children if both parents are single children."[1] This new policy will then be further relaxed nationwide.

This announcement is the first nationwide policy loosening of the One-Child Policy since 1980. This will lead to about one to two million additional new births in Mainland China every year, currently at 15 million births per year.[2]

As discussed earlier, the One-Child Policy led to the formation of the "4-2-1" Family, which is fundamental to the economic status of the China Ones. As China Ones are growing up to the age of being parents in the short future (about 0-5 years), they will be at the stage of making decisions for how many children they are willing to have. The new policy will bring the possibility of having a second child in their home. The decisions China Ones will make will directly influence their luxury shopping behavior: This new policy will encourage China Ones to buy luxury products for their children which will further enlarge the range of categories of their luxury shopping in the immediate future. With the rapidly increasing income and new luxury shopping focused products, this trend will lead to a new era of Chinese luxury market with China Ones as a young-to-middle age consumer segmentation.

THE TIGHTENING OF XI'S GOVERNMENT AND ITS POLICY

"Xi Jinping may have the most concentrated power of any Chinese leader since Deng Xiaoping," said Xiao Gongqin, a professor of history in Shanghai; "Politically, he has pursued an ideological tightening, because he wants to prevent the kind of explosion in political demands that could come in a relaxed environment. That's the biggest danger for any government entering a period of reform."[3]

One of the signs of the tightening of the new government's policy is the strong and rough policy against gifting to government officers, in order to control internal government corruption. " Most people thought that gifting would last for a while, but there is now a real government crusade against it...which in turn is affecting retailing, particularly in China's big government cities,"[4] said Jon Cox, an analyst at Kepler Capital Markets, who estimated that gift-giving accounted for around half of the luxury sold in mainland China.[5]

There are many China Ones who are affected by this new direction of policy – those who are working for the government as an officer or dealing with PR relationships with the government will have to watch out for the trends. The tightening of Xi's government policy will influence the income that the China Ones are getting as well as seriously reduce the gifting of luxury goods.

THE CHANGING TASTE – DYNAMIC OF CHINA ONE'S LUXURY SHOPPING BEHAVIOR
FROM PHYSICAL PRODUCTS TO EXPERIENTIAL PRODUCTS

Much media attention has currently been focused on the changing of Chinese luxury consumers' behavior; moreover, market analysts point out that the shift is related with the natural evolution of consumer habits and the shift in the realization of needs.

Shaun Rein, Managing Director of China Market Research Group in Shanghai said during his interview with the *New York Times* that a sign luxury shopping has slowed down due to the consumers re-prioritizing what they want to buy.[6] As the consumers are becoming more mature, they tend to try new categories of luxury products, particularly towards experimental luxury products such as luxury vacations and traveling. Yuval Atsmon, a principal of McKinsey & Co., said the growing luxury consumers' sophistication and the increasingly wide selection of available products as well as the quality of the service in luxury experiential products had resulted in a diversification of consumer spending.[7]

As younger, open-minded luxury consumers, China Ones are the first group interested in trying new luxury products. This "From Physical Products To Experiential Products" trend will lead the future strategy development towards Chinese luxury consumers, especially the China Ones.

FROM SHOPPING DOMESTIC TO GOING ABROAD

According to the United Nations World Tourism Organization, China's economy included $102 billion spent on travel abroad in 2012. The rise of incomes, combined with a need of relaxation through foreign travel, has fueled the Chinese luxury consumer's new shopping trend.

Scott Taber, a vice president at Four Seasons Hotels and Resorts, said his company was experiencing around 76 percent increase of travelers from mainland China over 2013.[8]

To market to these individual travelers from China, many global luxury brands are making marketing campaigns to attract Chinese travelers via websites and on-line advertising in China because luxury shopping is the "Thing to do" on almost every traveler's list.

Affluent and travel-hungry Chinese are increasingly buying overseas. About half of Chinese spending on luxury goods occurs outside the mainland, according to a study released in December by the consulting firm McKinsey. Si Jingnan, an engineer from Beijing, says he travels to the United States once or twice a year and takes a shopping list from relatives or friends.[9] "50 square meters in Paris could be much more meaningful now than having those same 50 square meters in China," said Mr. Bennahmias of Audemars Piguet.[10] This statement shows how important it is for the luxury brands to target traveling Chinese luxury consumers. Overall, according to Bain & Co. in 2013, Chinese luxury shoppers' spending has grown to 25 percent of the world total. Because a portion of the shopping was done abroad, it is proven that Chinese luxury consumers are the most powerful consumers in the world, not domestically, but globally.[11]

REVIEWING THE CONCEPT - WHAT HAS BEEN COVERED IN THIS BOOK
OBJECTIVE

This book studies China One's identity, value system, preferences and behaviors toward luxury shopping. The goal of this study is to understand the rapidly growing power of the China Ones and their consumption in the Chinese Luxury Market through primary and secondary research, aiding in the development of specific frameworks based on the data and insights.

PRIMARY RESEARCH

During primary research, the author got a clear understanding of the China One group's demographic and psychographic significance, as well as shopping behaviors toward luxury shopping. Based on classic frameworks and theory, LSEDP, a motivation-orientated segmentation, is created to a support luxury-marketing strategy toward China Ones.

SECONDARY RESEARCH

According to the secondary research, about 20 percent of the Chinese people are China Ones; in other words, about 250 million young people belong to this segment. It cannot be denied that the China One group is playing an increasingly important role in the modern society of China. In three to five years, China Ones will become the mainstream consumer of any product in China.

KEY TRENDS OF CHINA ONE'S LUXURY CONSUMPTION

Through primary and secondary research, there are several China One luxury shopping attitudes and outside factors that are not only bringing a new age of luxury but also are changing the rules of the game.

1. CHINA ONE'S NEW LUXURY CONSUMPTION VALUES:

The growing categories of luxury such as electronic products, experiential services (travel, spa, etc.), and automobile / yachting signal that China One's values are transitioning from owning to belonging, from extrinsic to intrinsic, as well as from conspicuous to meaningful. There are fundamental differences between traditional luxury products and luxury experiences, but there are lots of items that fall into the overlapping hybrid category, or a mix of the two.

Because of the historical background and unique family structure, China Ones value luxury more than consumers from any other areas of the world. These changes in values among luxury consumers in China in general are also a result of blurring the boundaries between luxury and mass-market items in China's market.

There are more and more mainstream brands beginning to market their products differently in China– they market themselves the same way as luxury brands. This trend of re-branding for the Chinese combined with the trend of the growing power of affordable brands will enlarge the market by introducing luxury lifestyles and values to many more potential consumers, especially China Ones.

2. THE NEW WAY OF LUXURY SHOPPING:

Chinese luxury consumption accounts for $156-169 billion.[12] Since China became a luxury hot-spot, consumers have shifted their shopping places from domestic to overseas. According to BCG's research, "About 42 percent of luxury goods bought by Chinese consumers are purchased on Mainland China; 33 percent are purchased in Hong Kong, Macao and Taiwan; and 25 percent are purchased in other foreign countries. Shopping is also the main expenditure for Chinese consumers outbound travel– 40 percent of their expenditure is on shopping, two percent is on accommodation, 19 percent is on meals and 19 percent is on entertainment and other expenses. Therefore, marketers must welcome these Chinese travelers who will buy."[13] This data shows how the trend of shopping abroad has shifted to influence future marketing strategy development.

3. NEW BUSINESS MODELS TOWARD CHINESE LUXURY MARKET:

There are many luxury brands and retailers that are changing their business models– licensing, co-branding, and on-line retailing.

By targeting younger luxury shoppers, the luxury marketers often explore new retail formats such as pop-up stores, special flagship stores and localized stores to increase the excitement of the brand among younger customers in China. Additionally, there are On-line-only retailers, such as Net-A-Porter, that have earned a lot of attention from the China One group.

FRAMEWORK DEVELOPMENT

Based on the segmentation and the re-creation of classic models [Maslow's Theory, Rogers's Diffusion of Innovation and VALS], the study has combined the primary and secondary research results together to further develop a LSEDP segmentation system to guide the strategy development towards China Ones luxury shopping behaviors. There are three steps to utilize this framework:

STEP ONE

According to research results, the China One's New Maslow Needs Diagram was developed for strategy building, which has been refined with fewer needs in the first two basic levels adding but more needs in the top three levels.

In addition, instead of having three levels listed as low to high, the China Ones' Hierarchy of Needs diagram has three horizontally distributed on the top of the triangle in order to emphasize the core need of Self-actualization as well as importance of Love and Social as well as Esteem needs.

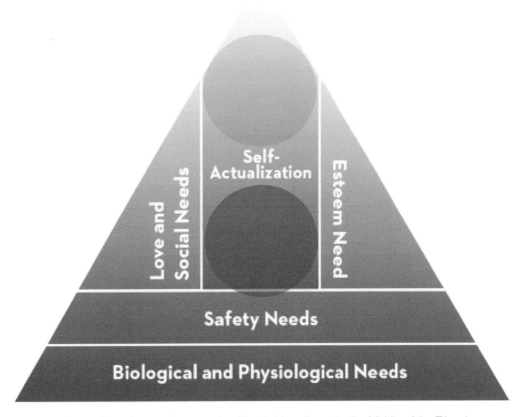

Figure 45 China One's Luxury Consumption Needs Move Down to the Middle of the Triangle

STEP TWO

According to the different levels of Needs from the China One's refined Maslow Needs Diagram, each of the marketing mix elements is placed with the similar level of the Needs matching the level of marketing elements from basic to advanced.

Figure 46 Marketing Mix Attributes Based on China One's Needs

STEP THREE

According to each element of the Marketing Mix – 4PS, strategies are developed targeted on China Ones' needs and wants.

Figure 47 Marketing Strategy Development based on China Ones' Needs

"PRODUCT" STRATEGY:

When targeting China Ones, the product's strategy should concentrate on developing unique products that stand out from the competition. Moreover, the reputation of the brand is also important for marketers to build in order to develop loyalty with their customers. The strategy should encourage the feeling of pride in ownership as a sign of a successful, high quality lifestyle.

"PRICE" STRATEGY:

When targeting China Ones, the pricing strategy needs to be built based on the cost of the product, the competitor's price, as well as the reputation of the brands. Luxury brands should focus on adding value to services as well as consumer relationship developing events to further build a long-term value adding marketing strategy.

"PLACE" STRATEGY:

With the growth of e-commerce and on-line shopping, consumers now can shop for anything they want 24/7. When targeting China Ones, the marketing strategy towards promotion needs to primarily understand the information channels, distribution channels, and payment methods. Therefore, marketing strategy toward Place needs to be considered as a whole because the overall brand's experience needs to be the same in order to deliver the same message to communicate in a timely manner with the consumer.

"PROMOTION" STRATEGY:

The marketing strategy towards Promotion needs to understand the deep motivation of the consumer's purchasing behaviors. From the brand, to the culture, then to the story behind it, marketers need to create a story-telling strategy that helps bridge the communication with China Ones, further helping them to build the emotional connections with the brand and its product.

STEP FOUR

Adding three elements to the 4Ps: people, policy, and perception, to develop an overall rounded strategy towards the China One group.

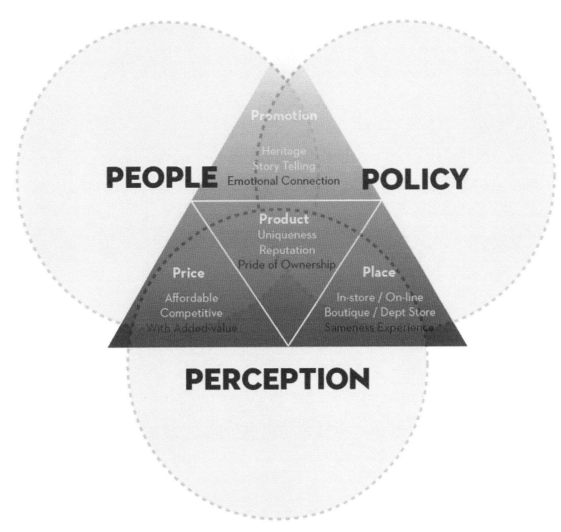

Figure 48 Marketing Strategy Development- The 7Ps

RECOMMENDATIONS IN-ACTION

Here are some recommendations for marketers developing strategies toward the China One group:

1. Understand the importance of the China One group as the most important consumer in the Chinese luxury market. This has about 250 million people, encompasses 20 percent of China's population meanwhile consumes about 40 percent of the Chinese luxury market. The China One group should not be mistakenly understood to be an ordinary young consumer segment because they have a different mind-set than other consumer groups in China. Nor are they like similar generations in other countries. The strategy needs to be directly tailored for them.

2. China Ones are looking for "质感"(zhi gan), the feeling of quality and texture, which requires the brands to push the overall communication into innovative and experiential levels, even with traditional luxury goods, and boost the luxury experiences as part of the product's added-value through storytelling.

3. Invest deeply to understand the China One group's segmentation. The LSEDP is a great supporting model to start with.

4. Consider new business models to maintain control while developing new distribution formats and attracting potential China One consumers. Become the "代购" (dai gou) by making the on-line store globally accessible to China Ones in order to help them get better price points to further increase sales toward China Ones.

5. Due to the unique information gathering abilities of the China Ones, availability of a variety of channels for luxury shopping, the brands need to create a cohesive presence with e-commerce, branding, blog and social media to improve their branding image and in order to better communicate to the China Ones.

WIN THE CHINA ONES, WIN THE WAR OF LUXURY GOODS

Combining with an increasing usage of social media, high involvement of technology as well as a maturing value system and related behaviors toward luxury shopping, the study of China Ones will not end here. China Ones will be the most important consumer group of all the luxury brands to study in the short and the long-term future.

The battlefield of luxury goods is no longer defined with geographic locations. Internet e-commerce, the trend of luxury shopping while traveling, dependent connections between areas, brands, and groups of people have taken the war into a new dimension. The competition among luxury brands has become the war of winning the heart of their consumers. In the war of leading the Chinese luxury market, winning the China Ones' hearts will ensure the victory on the battlefield at present as well as in the immediate future.

NOTES

1. The Third Force: The Psychology of Abraham Maslow, By Frank G. Goble.

2. Chris Buckley, "China to Ease Longtime Policy of 1-Child Limit," *The New York Times*, November 15, 2013, sec. World / Asia Pacific, accessed May 17, 2013, http://www.nytimes.com/2013/11/16/world/asia/china-to-loosen-its-one-child-policy.html.

3. Ibid.

4. Andrew Jacobs, "Xi Jinping Imposes Austerity Measures on China's Elite," *The New York Times*, March 27, 2013, sec. World / Asia Pacific, accessed May 17, 2013, http://www.nytimes.com/2013/03/28/world/asia/xi-jinping-imposes-austerity-measures-on-chinas-elite.html.

5. Raphael Minder, "Watchmakers Find Gold Rush in China Is Slowing Down," *The New York Times*, April 26, 2013, sec. Business Day / Global Business, accessed May 17, 2013, http://www.nytimes.com/2013/04/27/business/global/27iht-watch27.html.

6. Ibid

7. Sonia Kolesnikov-jessop, "Keeping Up With China's Changing Tastes," *The New York Times*, January 20, 2014, accessed March 17, 2014, http://www.nytimes.com/2014/01/20/fashion/keeping-up-with-chinas-changing-tastes.html.

8. Ibid.

9. Julie Weed, "Welcome, in Mandarin," *The New York Times*, November 11, 2013, sec. Business Day, accessed May 17, 2014, http://www.nytimes.com/2013/11/12/business/hotels-roll-out-welcome-mat-and-special-services-for-chinese-travelers.html.

10. Ibid.

11. Ibid.

12. Andrew Jacobs, "Xi Jinping Imposes Austerity Measures on China's Elite," *The New York Times*, March 27, 2013, sec. World / Asia Pacific, accessed May 17, 2013, http://www.nytimes.com/2013/03/28/world/asia/xi-jinping-imposes-austerity-measures-on-chinas-elite.html.

13. "BCG: Four Trends Driving the New Age of Luxury - Luxury Daily – Multichannel," accessed April 2, 2014, http://www.luxurydaily.com/bcg-four-trends-to-drive-retargeting-of-luxury-consumers/.

14. Ibid.

Appendix

A: INFORMATION OF "VALS"

According to "Strategic Business Insights"

VALS™ segments US adults into eight distinct types—or mindsets—using a specific set of psychological traits and key demographics that drive consumer behavior. The US Framework, a graphic representation of VALS, illustrates the eight types and two critical concepts for understanding consumers: primary motivation and resources. The combination of motivations and resources determines how a person will express himself or herself in the marketplace as a consumer.

VALS assigns individuals a VALS type on the basis of their responses to questions in the VALS Survey. VALS-typing populations of interest, such as customers or constituents, is the first step in a VALS approach to achieving strategic marketing and communication goals.

Using VALS provides clients with:

• A fresh perspective by effectively "putting them inside the head" of their customers

• Rich, customized, consumer profiles or persona

• Distinctive communication styles of their best targets.

Types of VALS segment:

1). Innovators. These consumers are interested in trying innovative technologies and creating their own products to benefit their life quality. They have higher incomes among all groups, and also have high self-esteem and abundant resources.

2). Thinkers. The consumers in this group have high resources and are a group of people motivated by ideals. They are mature, well educated and responsible. Their daily activities are centered at home, but they are well informed about new ideas and social change with the help of the Internet. They have higher incomes and are very practical and rational when they make purchasing decisions.

3). Believers. These consumers are the low-resource group of people who are motivated by ideals. Their conservative and predictable lives are centered on family and community.

4). Achievers. Consumers in this group are a high-resource group of people are motivated by achievement. They focus on successful careers and get satisfaction through their jobs. They love established products and services, which can help them to show off their success to peers.

5). Strivers. Consumers in this group are the low-resource group of people motivated by achievements. They have values very similar to Achievers but have less income and fewer resources. Style is very important to them, which helps them strive to emulate the people they admire.

6). Experiencers. Experiencers are consumers who are in the high-resource group motivated by self-expression. They are full of energy, which make them focus on exercise and social activities. They spend heavily on clothing, food, and technological products that emphasize new products and new services.

7). Makers. These consumers are in the low-resource group motivated by self-expression. They are focused on the familiar-family, work, and physical recreation and they have little interest in trying new technology or products. As consumers, they are more likely to buy lower priced, practical and functional products.

8). Survivors. This group of consumers has the lowest incomes and least resources. They are more likely to be the older generations who tend to buy products within the brands they are familiar with.

Elise 的论文调查问卷

首先感谢你帮我完成这份调研问卷，它将帮助我指出一条明确的方向，去寻找我要探索问题的答案。你的全部个人信息和问卷答案将不会被透露给商业单位进行骚扰型的促销行为，所有的资料信息只以数据模式存在并将完全的保密。

再次感谢你的帮助！

第一部分：我做我自己（介绍一下你自己吧）
我的名字是：

我是
○ 男生 ○ 女生

我目前住在

○ 北京	○ 上海	○ 重庆	○ 天津	○ 杭州	○ 武汉	○ 长沙
○ 广州	○ 深圳	○ 南宁	○ 贵阳	○ 海口	○ 石家庄	○ 哈尔滨
○ 郑州	○ 福州	○ 兰州	○ 南京	○ 南昌	○ 长春	○ 沈阳
○ 呼和浩特	○ 银川	○ 西宁	○ 济南	○ 太原	○ 合肥	○ 西安
○ 成都	○ 乌鲁木齐	○ 拉萨	○ 昆明	○ 澳门	○ 台湾	○ 海外
● 其他						

我的年纪是
○ 18~20 ○ 21-24 ○ 25-28 ○ 29-32

我是家里唯一的孩子么？ [单选题] [必答题]
○ 是
○ 不是

我的电子邮件是

我现在的职业是

让我告诉你我的穿衣风格（1-5，1 为贴近左边的描述，5 为贴近右边的描述）

	1	2	3	4	5	
时尚	○	○	○	○	○	经典
商务	○	○	○	○	○	休闲
华丽	○	○	○	○	○	低调
考究剪裁	○	○	○	○	○	简约剪裁
忠于特定品牌	○	○	○	○	○	尝试各种品牌
每日风格大体相同	○	○	○	○	○	风格多变

你最近有穿着/佩戴/使用任何奢侈品么?

○ 有

○ 没有

如果有，是什么、多少价格购买的?

第二部分：我买我喜欢(告诉我你是如何购物的？)

1. 你每月的收入是？(不包括父母提供的金额)

○ 0–500 元

○ 500–1000 元

○ 1000–1500 元

○ 1500–2000 元

○ 2000–3000 元

○ 3000–5000 元

○ 5000–8000 元

○ 8000 元以上

2. 你每月的消费总额是多少?

○ 0–500 元

○ 500–1000 元

○ 1000–1500 元

○ 1500–2000 元

○ 2000–3000 元

○ 3000–5000 元

○ 5000–8000 元

○ 8000–10000 元

○ 10000 元以上

3. 哪三个项目是你平均每月花费最多的?

| ○ 住房和房屋水电 | ○ 车贷或交通 | ○ 餐饮 | ○ 美容美发 | ○ 服装 | ○ 鞋子，包包和其他饰品 | ○ 电子产品 | ○ 电影,酒吧,KTV/旅行出游 | ○ 其他 |

4. 每月你会平均花费多少钱在时尚产品的消费上面?(包括服装鞋帽，包包及其他饰品，香水，化妆品等)

5. 每月你会平均花费多少钱在 奢侈 时尚产品上?

第三部分：我爱奢侈品（告诉我你对奢侈品的看法吧）

请告诉我什么是你认为的奢侈品？（定义或者列举品牌都可以）

1. 告诉我你为什么喜欢奢侈品？
- 奢侈品是高质量生活的标志
- 奢侈品是成功人士的必备标签
- 奢侈品是诠释个人品味的重要途径
- 奢侈品让人心情愉悦
- 奢侈品帮助我成为众人目光的焦点

2. 请选择你同意的说法
- 我欣赏一个品牌背后的品质和价值，而不是仅仅那个品牌的名字和知名度
- 一个奢侈品品牌不需要被所有人熟悉，只需要被它的忠实顾客喜爱和认同就足够了
- 我爱奢侈品，但是大多时候，我的经济能力很难负担得起
- 和购买奢侈品包包和衣服相比，我更愿意花费在豪华游轮，出国旅行，高尔夫，spa等"经历型奢侈品"上面
- 我非常务实，不愿意买价格超高的奢侈品，对于设计师品牌(CK,DKNY,Diesel...)倒是更加偏爱
- 只有那些被很多人熟悉的品牌才能被成为奢侈品牌
- 只有那些很少有人买的起的品牌产品，才能被成为奢侈品
- 因为我不喜欢show off（太张扬，高调），所以我不喜欢购买奢侈品
- 因为奢侈品价都很高，我会很小心的使用它们，甚至仅作为收藏而很少使用
- 当明星们都喜欢用某种奢侈品的时候，我做消费决定的时候，会比较愿意考虑购买同样品牌或款式的

3. 你购买奢侈品的动机是什么（不限于唯一选择）
- 奖励自己
- 善待自己，对自己好一些
- 为一些特殊场合佩戴，穿着用
- 享受高质量的生活
- 表现我的个人品味和价值
- 表现我的专业或社会地位
- 享受对奢侈品的所有权
- 由于工作需要
- 为了融入到我的社交圈子里
- 收藏，期待升值后卖出盈利
- 收藏，为了保值或
- 追求经典
- 张扬自己的个性和个人形象
- 希望自己时尚，与众不同
- 让自己更有自信，有魅力

4. 在你考虑购买奢侈品的时候哪 三个因素 是你考虑最重要的?

- ○ 高端品质，耐用时间长
- ○ 价格，折扣
- ○ 设计和造型
- ○ 材料和质地
- ○ 很好的售后服务
- ○ 长时间的保修期
- ○ 独特性，限量/特别版
- ○ 品牌的历史和文化
- ○ 环保性
- ○ 品牌的社会责任感
- ○ 店面设计，店内陈列和服务
- ○ 品牌认知度
- ○ 奢侈品流行程度
- ○ 明星的使用和推广
- ○ 欧洲/美国品牌的独有文化

5. 你认为在中国市场上，做的最成功的奢侈品品牌是哪一个?

6. 告诉我你最喜欢的奢侈品品牌是

为什么?

7. 你最喜欢的其他时尚品牌是哪一个?
奢侈品牌时装类

其他品牌时装类

包包和配件

鞋子

香水

手表首饰

眼镜、太阳镜

第四部分：我买我时尚（请分享你的奢侈品消费经验）

1. 去年你在奢侈品消费上面的花费是

2. 你最近的一笔消费是购买了什么产品？多少钱？

3. 你每年买几次奢侈品牌的产品？
- ○ 0 次
- ○ 1 次
- ○ 2 次
- ○ 3 次
- ○ 4 次
- ○ 5 次
- ○ 6 次-8 次
- ○ 9-10 次
- ○ 10 次以上

4. 在你所有的奢侈品中，你最喜欢的是哪一件？为什么？

6. 你消费的最多的奢侈品是哪 三项？
- ☐ 正装
- ☐ 日常服装
- ☐ 包包和配件
- ☐ 鞋子
- ☐ 香水
- ☐ 手表首饰
- ☐ 眼镜、太阳镜

7. 最近有想要购买的产品么？是什么呢？

8. 如果不考虑价格因素，你最想拥有的一件 时尚类奢侈品 是什么？

9. 告诉我你最难忘的一次奢侈品购物经历是在哪个品牌，购买了什么？

10. 你喜欢的购物方式是？
- ☐ 品牌专卖店
- ☐ 商场专柜
- ☐ 网上购买
- ☐ 出国亲自购买
- ☐ 国外代购

为什么？

3. 你每隔多久做一次关于奢侈品的调查，寻找喜欢的产品？

○ 每天
○ 一周多于一次
○ 每两周
○ 每月一次
○ 半年一次
○ 随机

4. 你从什么途径获取奢侈品相关的信息会让你想要试穿/试戴的冲动？

○ 我在喜欢的品牌网站上看见了新产品的广告
○ 我看到了网上消费者的评价和回馈
○ 我在除品牌网站外的其他网站看见了关于这个产品的广告信息
○ 我收到了朋友或家人的推荐
○ 我看到别人使用这个产品，觉得很不错
○ 我在杂志或报纸上看到了关于这个产品的文章或广告
○ 我看到了电视上的广告
○ 我在微博或豆瓣等网上交流平台看见了关于这个产品的信息或广告
○ 我逛街的时候在这个品牌的店里看到了实际产品的陈列
○ 我和销售聊过后，他/她推荐我购买这个产品
○ 我在这个品牌的产品目录里看见了这个产品

5. 什么因素会让你很想要买下你看到的这个奢侈品？

☐ 很符合我的个人品味
☐ 限时折扣
☐ 家人和朋友的极力推荐
☐ 很不错的赠品
☐ 限量版的设计
☐ 当下正在发生的流行趋势
☐ 成为 VIP 会员的资格
☐ 销售的服务很到位
☐ 我的朋友都买了这个产品
☐ 产品推广做的很到位，广告和宣传很引人入胜

6. 你经常是一个人逛奢侈品店并消费么？

○ 是，从调查资料到购买都是一个人拿主意
○ 不全是，先一个人去看，然后和朋友一起去买
○ 不全是，先一个人去看，然后和家人一起去买
○ 不是，和朋友一起去看，然后购买
○ 不是，和家人一起去看，然后购买

169

7. 当你在网上搜索关于奢侈品的信息的时候，你一般去哪个网站？

8. 你对于网上消费奢侈品的态度是？
- ○ 一点都不感兴趣
- ○ 有点兴趣
- ○ 一般
- ○ 很有兴趣
- ○ 极有兴趣

9. 你在网上消费过奢侈品么？
- ○ 有
- ○ 没有

如果有，你购买了什么？

什么时候购买的？

在哪个网站购买的？

你对产品满意么？
- ○ 满意
- ○ 不满意

10. 有没有什么奢侈品品牌是你很想消费但是在你居住的城市里面没有专卖店的？
- ○ 有
- ○ 没有

如果有，是哪个品牌？

Elise 再次谢谢你的支持~谢谢！
如果有任何问题和意见反馈，请由电子邮件联系我。

ABOUT THE AUTHOR

Elise Ran Wang (王然) is a practitioner-scholar who holds two Master degrees in Luxury Marketing and Design Management; She is an architect of marketing strategies and frameworks, an entrepreneur and a world-wanderer.

Her work explores a wide range of domains such as the dynamics of consumer behaviors and emergent marketing trends, brand strategies and organizational development, social network analysis, methods of contextual research and business model innovation. These topics are not applied in isolation, but are blended together to shape a powerful approach to discovering and creating original, human-centric solutions to the ever changing world.

Prior to undertaking multiple Master's degrees in the US, Elise spent several years in China on creative business development, events management, as well as brand strategy consulting. Now she aspires to leverage the full scope of her experiences to build frameworks that catalyze creative potential to help global brands and companies continue growth, especially in mainland China.

Made in the USA
Lexington, KY
23 September 2014